BLINKERS OFF

NEW FRONTIERS
IN FORM CYCLE ANALYSIS

CARY FOTIAS

EQUIFORM/THE XTRAS
23-48 Crescent Street
Astoria, NY 11105
equiform.com 866 374 3676

Published by Equiform LLC
website: www.equiform.com

First published in USA 2002
©Cary Fotias, 2002

ISBN 0-9715803-0-8

Library of Congress Cataloging in Publication Data available from the Library of Congress

Trademark Notices

Cover design by Dave Kitagawa

Printed by United Book Press, Inc

Contents

II   Blinkers Off – Exploring THE XTRAS   55

7   The New Pace Top   57

8   Distance Switches   85

9   Lightly Raced Horses   99

10 Turf Racing   109

11 Track Biases   147

Foreword

The publication of this book on Cary Fotias's handicapping methods is a landmark event in thoroughbred betting. As students of the racetrack know, I view racetrack betting as a financial market with two steps: determine the chance that various horses will finish first, second, third, fourth, etc and then wager intelligently on them where the odds are sufficiently better than chance to provide a betting edge. My own methods emphasize the wagering dimension, assuming that the public generates good estimates of the odds. Cary's approach provides methods to obtain more accurate odds than the public. By evaluating performance throughout the race, his numbers provide a good picture of *how* the horse ran a particular race. By looking at the pace and final numbers across races, one gains valuable insights into what the horse is likely to do in its next race. Then, by comparing these numbers for all horses in the race, one gets a full view of the race dynamics and possible scenarios.

Proper betting focuses on value plays for win, place and show and various exotic wagers. Several concepts utilized in stock market prediction are also applicable at the racetrack: moving forward replaces momentum, bounce replaces mean reversion, etc. The 2001 Kentucky Derby is a good example. Several horses looked like they were moving forward. At 10-1, Monarchos looked like a much better bet then Point Given at 2-1 since their numbers were comparable. So Monarchos was my major pick and led to profits when he ran the race of his life, finishing in under two minutes. The 2000 Breeders Cup Classic had the favorite Fusaichi Pegusus at 6-5, but Tiznow, at 9-1, had only slightly weaker numbers and looked like he was moving forward. With Cary's help, we also liked Giant's Causeway at 7-1, who was overlooked in the betting despite his two wins over Kalanisi, who had just won the Breeders' Cup Turf. So I played both of them across the board and in exactas. They went head to head during the entire stretch with Tiznow winning narrowly, benefiting from a spectacular ride from Chris McCarron. It was a terrific payoff and a very good value outcome. The overbet Fusaichi Pegasus, just like Point Given, finished out of the money.

The ability to establish accurate win probabilities is the key to successful handicapping, and **THE XTRAS** provide superior information that allows the handicapper to more precisely evaluate each horse's chance of winning. In addition, The Xtras are a powerful tool for owners and trainers looking to claim, privately purchase, or properly place their horses. As students of Cary's methods learn more about the myriad uses of The Xtras, their understanding of thoroughbred condition and performance will increase dramatically.

I have been going to the races, mostly the Kentucky Derby, Breeders Cup, Belmont Park, and Saratoga with Cary Fotias for the past ten years. I have authored several books on racetrack betting and been a consultant for a professional Hong Kong betting syndicate. As a critical academic, I do not believe that many racetrack betting systems work. As I watched Cary in his own betting and in the study of his numbers, I have become more and more convinced about the advantages they provide. The comprehensive information that The Xtras furnish allows a handicapper to visualize the possible outcomes of any given race. Then, one can focus on the plays with good chances to win relative to their payoffs. These methods are not a cookbook with simple recipes for what to do. Rather, they employ a vast array of useful data that, when properly analyzed, provides valuable hints as to what will happen in the race at hand. This is a most creative, entertaining and well-written book. Its publication will, in my view, make a major impact on the way races are analyzed and wagered on in the future.

Dr Z (Professor William T Ziemba)
December 2001

Dedication

For my wife, Mary, without whose unwavering patience and love, this book would have been 1,000,000 to 1.

Acknowledgments

The publication of this book and creation of **THE XTRAS** would not have been possible without the assistance and support of several friends. First, I would like to thank Ken L'Homme, whose belief in the product over the last ten years has been a constant source of inspiration. Ken also manages the company's web related issues. Next, John van Aken, more affectionately known as JVA, for his determination and organizational skills, and Buck Spurr, for his public relations work and magic tricks. Then, Roni Evron, who is not only an expert programmer, but is always there when I need him, and Bill Feingold, Bill Ziemba (Dr Z), and Richie Schwartz for their perceptive feedback during the design process.

Tony Alessandrini was instrumental in polishing the rough edges of the manuscript, Sandra Schwartz did a marvellous job of editing and preparing the final draft, and Steve Terelak was a trusted guide throughout the publishing process. I would also like to thank Ron Weinstock, Peter Arnold, Peter Rotondo, and Andrea Fotias for their insights and George Brice for managing the office.

And finally, thanks to my parents, Anne and Andy Fotias, who have always encouraged me to pursue my dreams.

Part I

The Theory

Chapter 1

Introduction

Horseplayers, if they are considered at all, are generally dismissed by society as a ragtag assortment of losers who live somewhere beyond the pale of respectability. This is because there is an assumption that horseplayers are compulsive gamblers and compulsive gamblers are invariably compulsive losers. No such derogation is aimed at those who make their money on Wall Street. Indeed, they are revered as wise investors, perceptive financiers or opportunistic venture capitalists. The reasons underlying this dichotomy are not easily explored or necessary to our undertaking. But it does point to a very important distinction between gambling and compulsive losing. Wall Street, unlike the racetracks, quickly weeds out the compulsive losers. The stakes are too high for them to stay in the game. Those who do flourish in the financial markets are serious investors who have confidence in themselves to make reasonable, fact-based decisions about how they invest and manage their money.

So it must be with successful horseplayers. To be a winning handicapper, three major ingredients are required:

- Developing and maintaining a winning attitude;

- Accessing and utilizing superior information; and

- Practicing a sound and prudent money management scheme.

These principles appear, in some variation or another, in every "How to Succeed" manual ever published. The fact that they have become clichéd does not mean they are not true. It does mean, however, that they are often overlooked or, worse yet, are not given the weight they deserve because they are so obvious.

A winning attitude is especially important when the fates are being unkind. A loss of confidence in one's abilities can be treacherous. When betting on the races becomes a roller coaster ride of conflicting emotions that rattle the faith of even the most devout believer, it is absolutely paramount that one maintains his equanimity. Like most things, this is much easier said than done. Nevertheless, the bettor who unravels and begins to doubt his skill invites catastrophe. A person who does not believe he can win, will not. It is as simple as that.

Managing one's money capably is wedded to cultivating a winning attitude. While it is true that if one succeeds in a task, one becomes more confident, it is equally true that when one's confidence is shaken by momentary adversity, it is extremely easy to lose one's discipline. And loss of discipline leads to foolish bets. No one is immune to "getting steamed" or "going on tilt". But the successful handicapper, like the professional Wall Street investor, quickly learns to control these destructive impulses.

It is the second principle though, accessing and effectively utilizing superior information, that is at the heart of **EQUIFORM**. Many variables affect the outcome of a horse race. Since all races are unique events, any one variable may dominate in certain situations. A horse's ability to handle a muddy track may be powerful in one situation but not another. Occasionally a trainer may be on a tear "first off the claim". Pace, distance, class, weight, surface, trainer and bias all contribute to the dynamics of a horse race. But a majority of the time, one factor supersedes all the rest. Form, or as we prefer to name it, **condition**, is the most consistent determinant of the outcome of any given race. Well-conditioned racehorses, ready to make a forward move, will normally defeat inherently faster horses that are not in shape to deliver a good effort. The challenge is to be able to identify these situations when they are concealed from the betting public.

The handicapping landscape has recently been inundated with all types of information. Whether it be trainer studies, four generation pedigrees, or trip notes, large quantities of data are easily accessible, especially by computer. However, it is burdensome to manage all the available information, and only the most dedicated players attempt it. **THE XTRAS** strive to distill as much pertinent information as possible while maintaining the focus on *condition* and *form cycle analysis*.

Equiform not only produces premium final time numbers, but also introduces our unique velocity-based pace numbers. The interrelationship of these two numbers (pace and final) and subsequent pattern analysis has enabled us to develop a superior methodology for analyzing condition and form cycles and predicting performance. Services that focus solely on final time are no longer in the vanguard. Equiform is the next step as The Xtras enable the handicapper to separate contenders that appear evenly matched on final numbers. Research oriented and continually seeking innovative approaches, Equiform will provide its users the ability to stay ahead of the crowd.

Chapter 2

The Whole Picture

A unique feature of **EQUIFORM** products is our proprietary internal fraction calculations. These numbers are extraordinarily useful. Just as one inning cannot create a baseball game or one color a painting (except at the Guggenheim), one number is usually inadequate for evaluating the events of an entire race. Several racing publications and track programs publish $\frac{1}{4}$, $\frac{1}{2}$ etc times for this reason. They are meaningful, but the challenge is to effectively use these often ignored times as part of an overall handicapping analysis.

During a racing season, a top thoroughbred may run only six to ten times. Less valuable stock may race anywhere from ten to thirty times (or fifty, in the case of our old New York pal Murray Garren). In its entire career, an animal may log only an hour or so of actual racing time. As an analogy, a single race might equate to one or two years on the job for a human being working 40 years. During an entire career, humans have good years and bad years - or in the financial markets, great minutes and horrible minutes. Generally, one year of performance does not give a complete picture of one's abilities. And yet in racing, one number is often used to judge a critical minute or two in the life of a thoroughbred. Equiform has long viewed this as a very shortsighted approach.

Recognizing the importance of the internal fraction calculations and interpreting how they predict a horse's likely performance are Equiform's distinguishing features. The relatively minimal amount of

real racing time a horse accumulates makes every part of the race important. Equiform's research has shown that valuable insights are gained
when specific segments of a race - the race within the race - are analyzed.
Understanding this information provides a much more accurate gauge
of a horse's current condition than can be gleaned from the usual fractions in other publications. Equiform's internal numbers paint a more
complete picture of a horse's racing experience.

Equiform's final number encompasses several key variables, a complex topic which will be more fully explored later. But, for starters,
Equiform's numbers will enable you to recognize how the animal's energy was distributed over a specific distance, thereby assisting you in
deciphering the horse's true potential in any given race.

All the nuances of horse racing cannot be reduced solely to numbers and, certainly, one number cannot tell the complete quantitative
or "scientific" side of the handicapping equation. There is definitely a
qualitative or "artistic" aspect to the handicapping puzzle that serious
participants welcome. By providing the scientific data that its research
has shown is pertinent, Equiform builds a unique and innovative "can-
vas" to which you add the color.

This blending of art and science is unattainable with selection sheets
or single number analysis. At Equiform, all our numbers are rigor-
ously scrutinized for validity, but we never underestimate the individual
player's ability to add a personal "artistic" flourish.

Chapter 3

The Education of a Horseplayer

Down on the Farm

I was born in Grand Rapids, Michigan, and attended the races for the first time when I was fifteen years old. But my interest in horse racing predated that initial foray by several years. I remember being about ten years old and enjoying the big races like the Kentucky Derby and the Belmont Stakes on television. Having a mathematical bent, I was also fascinated by the constantly changing numbers on the tote board. Even at that young age, I sensed there was a relationship between those numbers and what happened on the track. I was curious and wanted to understand it. So when my mom agreed to drive a friend and me to Detroit for a Tiger's night game (another passion of mine), I persuaded her that we might as well make a day of it. If we left in the morning, we would have plenty of time to take in the races at Detroit Race Course before heading out to Tiger Stadium. She agreed, and so it was that on a magic day in 1968, armed with my Kelco-Class-Calculator, I placed and won my first bet. Actually my mom placed the bet, but it was all my action - two dollars to show and a sixty cent profit.

Some of my friends shared my interest and, during our first period algebra class, we would trade insights about the day's upcoming races. At the time, *The Detroit Free Press* featured a handicapper who used the pseudonym Charlie Buck. He would start each spring with an imaginary bankroll of $500 and unbounded optimism. Unfortunately for his followers though, by mid summer all he had left was his optimism. But imaginary bankrolls are easy to come by, so "old Charlie" replenished and finished out the season.

My friends and I wondered if we could not do as well as Charlie Buck or his cohort at the paper, "Al Speed", and the other public racing cognoscenti. Staking ourselves to $500 apiece, we made our selections and compared our results with those of the pros. Amazingly, at the end of the season in December, our bottom lines were as good as and sometimes better than theirs. I realized that something was terribly out of kilter when a bunch of high school sophomores were as skilled (or more accurately, as unskilled) in picking winners as the putative experts.

Then came the mail order phase. Convinced that there had to be a system that would take into account all the variables in a race and reduce them to some comprehensive formula, I spent the next several years sending away for scores of methods. Do Norris Strauss, Lawrence Voegele or post office boxes in obscure Nevada towns ring a bell? Since most had a money-back guarantee, I culled what was useful and returned the bulk of them for a refund.

Then, while in the Grand Rapids public library one day, I came across a copy of Tom Ainslie's *Complete Guide to Thoroughbred Racing*. The snag was that I couldn't check it out. It was a reference book with metal strip on it which precluded anyone from sneaking it out the front door without triggering the detector. It was only a minor problem for an enterprising horseplayer. Suspecting that library employees must have another way out, I lingered one night until one of them left. Stealthily, I followed him down a few flights of a remote staircase. It led directly to the parking lot outside. I returned the next day and absconded with my prize. For the next few days, I devoured Ainslie. And, just for the record, I returned the book when I was finished.

Over the years, it gradually dawned on me that while handicapping had a mathematical aspect, it was an art as well. There were too many variables to quantify with anything approaching scientific accuracy. Consequently, relying on a formula or a fixed methodology would always be limiting. Applying a more eclectic approach would offer the best chance for long-term success.

Morning Workouts

Sometime in my late teens, after the usual initiation rites, I recognized two factors were paramount if I were someday to beat the races:

1. confidence in my own selection process; and

2. getting "value" for my wagering dollar.

Confidence comes from success, but is most needed when things aren't going well. If a strategy is logically conceived and reasonably executed, it makes no sense to discard it in a fit of emotional second guessing. No one gets it right all the time. And in this game, getting it right a fraction of the time is enough to prosper. That is why receiving value for your dollar is so important. Understanding when and why the price on a certain horse is too big is a far greater skill than merely picking winners.

I originally employed a rather crude selection process based on trips and value. I'd look for races where at least two, and preferably three or more, entrants had run within a few lengths of each other in the recent past. Even though I may not have seen the previous races, it seemed intuitively logical that racing luck could have made a few lengths difference in their respective performances. (Intuitively logical is an oxymoron whose meaning will only be really understood by hard core gamblers, a few random poets and anyone who has ever been passionately in love). In any event, when these animals would match up again, I would back the longer priced horse(s).

One trio of horses stands out in my memory. In the 1970s at Hazel Park, Kentucky Dew, Wichita Dancer, and Jerri Prince seemed to meet every couple of weeks in a starter handicap series. Kentucky Dew (who had only one eye) was a crowd favorite and would usually go off between 3/2 and 2/1, Wichita Dancer between 2/1 and 3/1, and Jerri Prince from 6/1 to 14/1. Jerri Prince wasn't quite as good as the other two, but was noticeably undervalued by the betting public. I estimated that if he were able to win just 20% of the time, a result I believed likely, I'd show a handsome profit. He did, and I was nicely rewarded - not because I picked the winner, but because I saw the value in placing the wager.

Over the next few years, my education continued on a sporadic basis. I read a book by Robert Dowst, and *Horse Sense* by Burton Fabricand, in which he elucidated his law of maximum confusion. There was also *Eliminate the Losers* by Bob McKnight and another one of Ainslie's books. I wound up buying Ainslie's private method and eventually, for $100, a mechanical spot play method from a good guy named Steve Duma. Duma was unique in that not only did he guarantee a profit over any series of a hundred races, but he also made the incredible offer of refunding any losses that might have occurred over those races as long as you could prove it by identifying the track(s) and presenting the losing tickets. Duma's was the first spot play system in which I really had any confidence. It consistently showed a profit. A major drawback, though, was that the plays were infrequent and mostly limited to older horses and geldings.

Then came a revelation. Andy Beyer's *Picking Winners* broke fresh ground. New avenues like trainer patterns, track bias, paddock inspection, and variant-adjusted speed figures were analyzed. Never before had such methods and theories been espoused in print. A couple of years later, Steve Davidowitz, one of Beyer's mentors, published *Betting Thoroughbreds*. Davidowitz had some insightful concepts like key races. Meanwhile, down in the East Village, Len Ragozin was meticulously cranking out his "sheets" for a select clientele. Although in nascent form, the renaissance in handicapping had arrived.

Early Preps

Poets, philosophers and barroom sages have all marveled at the fact that the human condition is so rife with contradictions. Competition and cooperation are antithetical concepts, but who can deny that both are essential human drives? Handicapping the races is an excellent example where these two disparate impulses blend together harmoniously. Betting on the races is about winning someone else's money. There is nothing more cutthroat. But at the highest levels, it is also an intellectual pursuit, trying to understand a game that defies mastery. And humans, joined in a common goal, invariably cooperate. So while it is that experts may prefer not to share information or insights on a particular race, they will enthusiastically discuss the theories that led to those insights. Some even publish their ideas. I have read most of the available material on handicapping — from Ragozin to Sartin, Ainslie to Ziemba, and hundreds in between. I am indebted to them all. Their works were my jumping off point.

While developing my theories about handicapping, I labored at many different jobs – driving a taxi, washing dishes, playing poker, getting an MBA, and trading foreign currencies on Wall Street, to name a few. After a prolonged effort, I assimilated Beyer's speed figure concepts and began making my own numbers each night after work. It was laborious to construct par time tables, beaten length adjustments and all the rest. But the hardest part was just making all the speed figures. I didn't really have time to do the job properly. This in turn detracted from my enjoyment of the total racing experience. I also realized that to win consistently I had to put in more work than my schedule permitted. As a result, for a few years, I gave up playing the game seriously. I continued to dabble for recreation, not losing, but not winning either. My intellectual pursuit of understanding the game was on hold.

When I moved to New York City in 1986, my apartment was around the corner from an an upscale OTB parlor, the Inside Track. Contrary to the speculation of some of my friends, that was not the sole reason I bought the co-op. But it was serendipitous. On my visits there, I occasionally noticed, scattered on the floor, scraps of paper containing the names of horses followed by a bunch of numbers. I asked a couple of the regulars what they were. Reluctant at first to talk about the "sheets", they eventually took me into their somber confidence, speaking in a tone that one might use when discussing where Jimmy Hoffa is actually buried. This was special information they were revealing.

I was skeptical at first about the usefulness of the "sheets" and disagreed with some of the fundamental ideas they represented. However, I realized that for $30 a day, I could use these figures instead of making my own. I could now concentrate on the two aspects of the game that most intrigued me, handicapping and wagering. The pursuit had begun again.

I used the "sheets" for several years. Gradually, I decided that their value was limited. Their major strength lies in delineating the form cycle of a horse. Their numbers do not represent final times, or even adjusted final times, but rather "effort" or "energy expended". There is no indication of the varied circumstances under which the figures were earned. They do not capture the dynamics of a race. Horse races are not conducted in a vacuum. Each entrant in a race contributes a unique set of characteristics, some quite powerful, that impact on all the other contestants. This applies to a horse with a minimal chance to win as well as the real contenders. The interrelationship and reflexive nature of these traits constitute the specific race dynamic.

EQUIFORM directly addresses this often neglected and misunderstood topic. It is my hope that the ideas and theories explored in this book will help you in your own challenge to master the game.

New Frontiers

Having accurate data is the bedrock of successful handicapping. But collecting the "right" data and understanding its true impact on the final result are what distinguish the excellent handicapper. At one time, the "sheets" were a revolutionary tool, providing superior information to a limited clientele. Certainly, there is no denying that they were a major force in determining the odds in New York. I became quite adept at using them in combination with some nuances adopted from other sources. Such things as trainer patterns, biases, breeding and pace were factored into my final selections. I was winning consistently, but was curiously unsatisfied.

I mentioned before that I had read quite a lot of the published material regarding handicapping. I studied the pace theories of Mahl,

Sartin, Brohamer and Taulbot to name a few. They all had something of value, but I detected flaws in each of the various approaches I examined. Clearly, no system or method is perfect or even close to perfect. I believed, however, that there existed a way to synthesize all I had learned into an approach that would enable me to analyze thoroughbred condition from a new perspective. I just had to find it.

I experimented with different techniques, trying to merge data, style, and theory into a unified, consistent model. In early 1991, I finally developed an information set and methodology that looked promising. Around the same time, I hit a sizable Pick Six. This enabled me to take the time to build a model, which included my proprietary formulas and algorithms, and to display the output in a user-friendly format. It took a year-and-a-half to get the job done, but finally in the fall of 1992, I had a workable prototype.

The results were gratifying. Recognizable patterns in the numbers that predicted an improving or a declining performance emerged with absolute clarity. Because these patterns were not evident to the crowd or even to the "sheet" players, I had a big advantage in New York. I also had similarly positive results when I branched out to other circuits.

A couple of years ago, I decided to cover almost all North American tracks. The costs associated with adding several new tracks, and the man hours necessary to preserve the integrity of my numbers (I just don't have the stamina to put in 20 hour days anymore), has made it desirable to also sell the data rather than rely exclusively on wagering.

Currently, I don't have the luxury of spending six to eight hours a day handicapping and making odds lines. I still peruse twenty to thirty races a day, but only bet when The Xtras pinpoint outstanding plays. Consequently, rather than play the "churn" game, I bet rather strongly on a few select races. This style has more day-to-day volatility, but is much less taxing and allows me to spend more time on research. My intellectual pursuit continues.

Chapter 4

First Principles

Thoroughbred Condition

Thoroughbreds are prima donnas. Why wouldn't they be? For centuries, they have been bred exclusively to race. Weighing around a thousand pounds with an almost rigid back and spindly legs that seem insufficient for the task, these magnificent animals, with jockeys astride, travel significant distances at speeds sometimes exceeding forty miles per hour. Their genes, shaped by human intervention, allow them to outperform the rest of their species in ways not anticipated by nature. They are truly the elite of *equus cabullus.*

But the tendencies of ancestry are not easily ignored. At their core, thoroughbreds are herd animals. On ancient grassy plains, where predators lurked everywhere, survival depended on staying close to the pack. If a horse moved too far ahead or lagged too far behind, it was easy prey. Still, some horses, more courageous or with a stronger will to dominate, are unafraid to lead the pack. Prizing this trait as an indicator of racing success, some keen buyers of thoroughbreds will delay major purchases until having the chance to see a yearling romp in the fields with its peers.

The start of the race is the most stressful event for many thoroughbreds. Some have to be schooled over and over again on getting in and getting out of the starting gate. From a standing position, the horse's hind feet drive backward and downward, while the horse's front end rises off the ground. This initial backward thrust enables it to hurl itself out of the gate. It is at this instant that the animal is in a precarious situation. Should the horse lose its balance or the ground break beneath him, the risk of an injury is increased. Assuming a clean break, horse and rider must now navigate their way through a pack of other furiously competing animals, all of them anxious to establish their own position. For these reasons, horses not in top racing condition often hurt themselves in the gate or in the early portion of the race. Even if they avoid physical injury, those not up to the challenge have considerably impeded their chances of winning.

Some handicappers minimize or ignore poor performances out of the gate, fallaciously reasoning that the explosion of energy at the outset is not that important. While **EQUIFORM** recognizes that some animals are perennially slow starters (due perhaps to an early negative experience), we believe that substandard gate performances suggest an underlying problem. Horses in proper condition ought to be able to handle the rigors of the start.

Horses that are feeling good and are well-conditioned most often exhibit their improved form in dirt races in the early segments. The ability to run faster in the most stressful part of the contest is usually a signal of an impending improvement in an upcoming race. How big an improvement depends on several factors, the most important being the acumen of the trainer and his ability to place his horse in a spot where it has a legitimate chance to win. Turf racing, on the other hand, involves a different set of dynamics. Here, an improvement in finishing ability is a likely indicator of readiness.

If a horse is entered in a race where the dynamics of the event allow it to distribute its newfound energy reserves effectively, it will deliver a superior performance, sometimes a lifetime best. Oftentimes, even when the dynamics are not ideally suited to a horse, an improved effort is probable. Recognizing these betting opportunities when others do not is fundamental to successful handicapping.

Pace

Much ado has been made about pace handicapping in the last decade. From the Sartin methodology and its proponents (Brohamer, Hambleton, et al) to Bloodstock Research, to Henry Kuck, and several others, pace numbers have sprouted up like wildflowers. In our opinion, the Sartin people have made the most significant discoveries. Although velocity-based pace numbers had been around awhile (via Huey Mahl for example), the Sartin crowd did some original work by creating and analyzing several types of pace ratings, studying energy distribution, developing track models, and bringing the whole process together with a well-defined decision model.

The problem with the Sartin approach is that the user is required to select a "representative" pace line for each horse in the race before proceeding with the next steps of the decision model. This appears to be shaky foundation, and the Sartin people themselves admit that selecting the right pace line takes a lot of practice. They go on to say that "when the difficulties involved have sorted themselves out, the correct pace lines will *loom* off the page." We wonder. A more serious flaw is their rationale of using one isolated performance to predict a future outcome. This disregard for the current form cycle of the horse (or the form cycle from which the pace line was selected), does not allow for a comprehensive evaluation of the horse's expected performance *today*. Only by looking at the animal's overall development can a true model of **condition** be created.

Thoroughbreds are bred to run, and it is not as easy as one might think to ration their energy. To begin with, all horses are individuals, and in the early stages of their racing careers, they are usually required to adapt to a variety of situations (dirt, turf, sprints, routes, off tracks, etc). As human runners have distinct preferences (Carl Lewis liked sprints while Jim Ryan preferred routes), so do the majority of racehorses. In fact, certain sprinters may handle seven furlongs better than six, or a router might love a mile-and-an-eighth, but just can't get ten furlongs. Conformation, pedigree, and other individual nuances all play a role in determining these preferences. Trainers continually experiment with their younger stock in an effort to discover what distance and surface is most suitable for each one. Rare indeed is the animal that can handle all distances and surfaces with equal aplomb.

We are now ready to commence our discussion of pace. Before we analyze the effects of pace on a horse race, and how it can assist us in solving the riddle of condition, first think of the idea in terms of your own daily activity. We've all probably said at one time or another "I've got to pace myself" or "I'm burning the candle at both ends." When we try to do too much work too quickly, or work around the clock without resting, our energy becomes depleted. Both our physical and mental apparatus begin to feel the strain and, until replenished, our performance suffers.

Thoroughbreds react to these same forces, and once we become cognizant of this, we begin to see them for the living, breathing creatures they are, rather than a bunch of numbers in the *Racing Form*. Ask a horse to expend too much energy early in a race, and it won't have much left for the finish (it didn't pace itself). Make a horse run at peak capacity a few times without the proper rest and recovery period, and you'll likely end up with an unhappy animal, often subject to injury (burning the candle at both ends). Racehorses aren't as stupid as some people think. One of the reasons older geldings are such consistent performers is that they know how fast they can run without hurting themselves. Younger animals, unaware of their own capabilities, are more prone to serious mishaps.

Most dirt races in North America, especially sprints, are experiences in *deceleration*. Next time you see a horse closing three lengths in the stretch, remember he is more likely just slowing down more slowly than the rest of the field. His "stretch move" is somewhat of an illusion. Consider the leader's normal fractions for a six-furlong race at your local track. They probably look something like this:

Horse A's fractions   22.7   46.3   1:11.7

(Throughout this book, we will use tenths of a second in our examples. Although most racetracks now time to the nearest one-hundredth of a second, and we use this data when available, tenths are sufficient for this discussion).

Let's assume the winner (Horse A) went wire to wire and look at the individual quarter times. It went the first quarter in 22.7, the second quarter in 23.6 (46.3 - 22.7), and the last quarter in 25.4. *Each subsequent quarter was run more slowly than the opening quarter*, with the last quarter being almost three seconds slower than the opening one.

Now, let's assume another animal (Horse B) is three lengths back after the first quarter, still three back at the half-mile call, and rallies off the pace for a dead heat with the frontrunner. Using the crude approximation of one length equals 1/5 second (the time value of one length varies at different rates of speed), Horse B's quarterly splits would be 23.3, 23.6, and 24.8. So, even though it gained three lengths in the final quarter, it was still travelling slower than it was in the opening segment.

How about a big closer? Well, let's say Horse C was twelve behind at the quarter, eight back at the half, and rallies for a triple dead heat with the other two horses. Its first quarter would be 25.1, its middle split 22.8, and its final quarter in 23.8. Horse C gained eight lengths in the final quarter, but still ran that segment a full second slower than the middle quarter. This type of deceleration at some point in the race is the norm in almost all sprints run on the dirt.

In dirt route races, the deceleration tends to be more gradual. Turf racing is a whole different ballgame, where the ability to accelerate late in the race (after the sometimes glacial early splits) is essential.

Velocity

Velocity is the rate per unit of time at which an object moves in a specified direction. Pitchers who throw heat are said to have "good velocity". Speeding drivers snagged by state troopers with radar guns and mirrored sunglasses might be said to have "too much velocity". Velocity simply measures distance over time, whether it's ninety-nine miles per hour (excellent speed for a fastball, not prudent on the Long Island Expressway), or fifty-five feet per second, the general speed of a competitive thoroughbred.

Feet per second (ft/sec) is the velocity measure we use in constructing our figures. Let's return to the first quarter of our imaginary race where the early leader (Horse A) ran the first quarter in 22.7 seconds. Its first quarter velocity in feet per second equals 1320 feet (a quarter mile) divided by 22.7 seconds, which equals 58.150 ft/sec. Remember, this is its average velocity during the first quarter. At certain points in the quarter, it is running faster than the average and, at other times, slower. As it leaps out of the gate from a standing start, the horse first overcomes inertia and then accelerates dramatically to reach full racing speed after about an eighth of a mile.

For the mathematically inclined, if this acceleration were constant, we could calculate its speed at any given point in the quarter (instantaneous velocity) by using differential calculus. But the acceleration is not constant. Sooner or later the horse levels off, and usually begins to decelerate later in the race. When the horse hits the turn, new factors come into play. How tight is the turn? How steeply is it banked? Does the animal's normal motion and physique allow it to negotiate different types of turns with the same agility? These are all difficult variables to quantify precisely. Anyone who tells you he can reduce all of this to one perfect "energy number" probably has a bridge in Brooklyn that he can let you have real cheap. What we can do is use the available data to produce reliable figures that allow us to make sound judgments concerning a horse's current condition. Chart-callers have a tough job and sometimes make mistakes. For that reason, we confirm our data with multiple sources, including personal observation at some tracks.

These raw velocity figures are the building blocks for all of our numbers, and they are adjusted for wind, turns, and our proprietary daily track variants. The key difference between our numbers and most of the others is that our figures are based on actual velocity, not projected final or fractional times.

Ground Loss

We make no adjustments in our numbers for *ground loss*, and believe it is overemphasized by certain prominent figure-makers. While the "sheet" players are busy wondering if a horse with a 19 from an inside post can beat a horse with a 17 breaking from the outside, they would be better served by paying more careful attention to any prevailing bias or other nuances. That is not say that ground loss isn't relevant, but rather that it has to be related to bias, the physics of a particular turn, and the horse's inside/outside proclivities. Horses with good early speed often are able to save ground and create their own luck. Downgrading these animals and upgrading horses going wide on the turn(s) is no better than making no adjustments at all. In either case, further analysis is necessary, and if there is a prevailing outside bias, making a ground loss adjustment up front can be very misleading.

For example, the 1991 Champagne Stakes for two-year-olds was contested over a Belmont surface that had been playing to outside closers for several days. Tri To Watch made the preferred move on the outside to win the race earning, if memory serves, a Ragozin 9. Meanwhile, Pine Bluff, stuck on the dead rail, was "rewarded" with a 15, essentially being penalized for saving ground, while Tri To Watch was earning bonus points going seven wide. Not only was this a misrepresentation of reality, but that 9 of Tri To Watch skewed the subsequent analysis of his development. As a three-year-old, he probably "circled" back toward that 9, but I don't recall if he ever got through it. The reality was that he didn't run a 9 in the Champagne. The ground loss adjustment coupled with an extreme bias had produced an inflated figure. Pine Bluff, although finishing third, had run a much better race than apparent and went on to capture the 1992 Preakness.

While ground loss adjustments solve the geometry of a turn, they don't deal with the physics involved. The circumference of a circle is $2\pi r$ (where π is roughly 3.14 and r is the radius of the circle). A turn is basically a semi-circle with a circumference of πr. Therefore, for every foot a horse is out from the rail, it must travel an additional π (or 3.14) feet. If we assume each running path is three feet wide, then each path out from the rail costs a horse about 10 feet, or roughly one length, per turn. That may get you an A on your geometry exam, but the next class is physics. How steeply is the turn banked? If graded properly, horses in the outside paths will have to spend less energy to hold their lanes than horses on the inside, as they have less centrifugal force to overcome. The ability to change leads effectively, the willingness to run inside of horses, and the general physical characteristics of the horse also come into play.

Expert contract bridge players, when defending a hand, are familiar with the adage "only give count when it counts". Otherwise, they may help the declarer more than their partner. The same applies to ground loss. "It only counts when it counts".

The great Forego thrilled racetrack crowds with his sweeping outside moves on the turn. To suggest he would have run faster by staying on the rail would be the height of folly. Without fully addressing the mechanics of the turn and conjuring up vectors, angular velocity, and displacement, no one really knows how different horses will handle different turns. Trying to quantify something so intangible hardly seems relevant.

What is relevant is realizing that certain horses like certain courses, another concept the "sheet" players have been reluctant to accept. This phenomenon can be a function of the racing surface, the turns, the altitude, or the local water supply to name a few.

In summary, be judicious in your appraisal of ground loss and give more credence to biases and track-to-track preferences.

Chapter 5

THE XTRAS

A New Approach

THE XTRAS are the definitive handicapping tool for evaluating thoroughbred performance and form cycles. They will allow you to interpret "the race within the race" and focus on condition angles overlooked by the public and other figure players. At a glance, you will be able to isolate horses with "hidden" moves. On each page of The Xtras, the last three years of a horse's performance are presented. The **final numbers** are graphed in the larger area of each yearly column, and the extra numbers are to the right. The number in parentheses ( ) is always the four furlong or **pace number**. If a dirt race was longer than six furlongs, the smaller number to the left of the pace number is the six furlong **turnback number**. In dirt sprints only, the **two furlong number** is to the right of the pace number.

All our numbers are hand crafted and velocity-based. They are adjusted for wind, weight, track configurations and our proprietary track variants. The graphed final numbers are reported in 1/4 point increments, while the extra numbers are rounded to whole numbers. The higher the number, the better the performance. The length value of one point varies at different distances. As a rough guide, one point is about one length at four furlongs, 1-1/2 lengths at six furlongs, 2 lengths at a mile, and 2-1/2 lengths at ten furlongs.

Weight is already factored into previous races. If contenders are not carrying equal weight today, credit horses carrying lower weight by 0.20 "final number" points per pound (that is, five pounds = one point).

To better understand the information presented on The Xtras, let's take a look at Affirmed Success (page 29) as he appeared in the seventh race at Belmont Park on July 4, 2001. A detailed legend for The Xtras appears on page 28. We will use Affirmed Success to illustrate some terms and symbols.

The race number, track, date, distance and surface appear near the upper left-hand corner, and the horse's assigned weight (121) to the right of its name.

As a five year-old (age at top of the columns), Affirmed Success raced six times. In early May of that year at Aqueduct (track code AQ), he ran an (82) pace number, a 79 two-furlong number, an 80 turnback number, and an 81" final number. In the last race of his 5yo season, he ran an (83) pace number, a 77 turnback number and a 78+ final number on a muddy (\) track. The final number of 78+ is in darker print, denoting a route race (one mile or longer).

The pace number is always in parentheses and represents four furlong velocity at all distances. As you will see, this number is the most important one to use in conjunction with the final number for evaluating condition. The turnback number represents six-furlong velocity in dirt races longer than 3/4 of a mile and appears to the left of the pace number.

In his fourth race as a six year-old, Affirmed Success ran on the grass (= preceding the final number) in early August at Saratoga (track code SR). He ran a (66) pace number, a 78" final number in a route on a good (ˆ) turf course and won (w) the race.

Two-furlong numbers only appear in dirt sprints and are to the right of the pace number. Turnback numbers only appear in dirt races. In grass races, the equal sign (=) also appears to the right of the pace number for easier identification. All off track symbols appear to the left of the final number.

If a sprint (light print) has a turnback number, the race was longer than six furlongs but less than one mile.

A full list of two letter track codes is available at www.equiform.com.

If you need further assistance with the notation or symbols on The Xtras, call our toll free number at 1-866-EQIFORM (374-3676).

We believe that sometimes less is more. Rather than clutter The Xtras with symbols denoting equipment changes, class, medication, trainer changes, etc, we recommend you use other information sources such as the *Daily Racing Form* in conjunction with The Xtras. It astounds me when I see Ragozin users analyzing races without the *Form* or other data. For example, how can they possibly judge the pace scenario without knowing the running styles of the participants? Oh, I forgot, Ragozin and his disciples believe that pace is just a minor annoyance in predicting race outcomes.

In any event, the user-friendly format of The Xtras will allow you to quickly identify the major contenders and evaluate condition and form cycles with more confidence. The Xtras add value to every ticket and offer you a better way to the winners' circle.

LEGEND

THE XTRAS are the definitive handicapping tool for
evaluating thoroughbred performance and form cycles.

THE XTRAS will allow you to interpret "the race within
the race" and focus on condition angles overlooked
by the public and other figure players. At a glance,
you will be able to isolate horses with "hidden" moves.

On each XTRA page, the last three years of a horse's
performance are presented. The **final numbers** are graphed in
the larger area of each yearly column, and the extra numbers
are to the right. The number in parentheses ( ) is always
the 4 furlong or **pace number**. If a dirt race was longer
than 6f, the smaller number to the left of the pace
number is the 6f **turnback number**. In dirt sprints only, the
two furlong number is to the right of the pace number.

All our numbers are hand crafted and velocity based. They
are adjusted for wind, weight, track configurations, and our
proprietary track variants. The graphed final numbers are
reported in 1/4 point increments, while the extra numbers
are rounded to whole numbers. The higher the number, the
better the performance. Weight is already factored into
previous races. If contenders are not carrying equal weights
today, credit horses carrying lower weight by .20 "final
number" points per lb.

SYMBOLS	TRACK CODES AND OTHER INFO
+ 1/4 point	two letter track codes on left
" 1/2 point	(see EQUIFORM.COM for list)
- minus 1/4 point	
	M in final number column
> wet fast	denotes missing race(s)
^ good	
/ sloppy	last race at top of right column
\ muddy	
< slow	age at top of yearly columns
+ heavy	
: frozen	weight at right of horse's name
= turf	
^= good turf	
.= yielding turf	**DISTANCE CODES**
:= soft turf	
+= heavy turf	light italic < 6f 70
*= hard turf	light 6f - 7-1/2 f 70
	bold 8f - 9-1/2 f **70**
	bold italic 10f or longer **70**

w   won race
( )   no pace number calculated
--   no final number calculated
xx   did not finish/eased

EQUIFORM™ Pg: 65   **AFFIRMED SUCCESS   (121)**   THE XTRAS ™

7TH BEL JULY 4 - 1 MILE TURF

	5	6	7
D e c			
N o v	AQ \78+w 77 (83)	AQ 79 73 (77)	
O c t	GP 72+ (81) 81	CD =79- (67) =	
		BE =78+ (71) =	
S e p	SR 80+ 81 (87) 83	WO =77 (68) =	
A u g			
		SR =^78"w (66) =	
J u l	BE 80- 79 (83) 79	BE =^78w (70) =	-->
J u n			
M a y	BE 78- 78 (86)		BE \78"w 78 (84) 80
A p r	AQ 81" 80 (82) 79	AQ 79" 77 (77) 84	
M a r			
F e b		LR 82-w 76 (81) 75	
J a n			

Chapter 6

General Principles

Now that we've covered the basics and outlined some of the theory behind **THE XTRAS**, it's time to elaborate on some general handicapping principles. A clear understanding of these general principles is necessary to most effectively use the information on The Xtras.

As it enters the starting gate, each horse has a certain amount of energy available to distribute during a race. How it distributes that energy is a function of several key variables.

1. the horse's particular running style

2. the pace demands of the race

3. the distance

4. the surface

5. the bias (if any)

6. the jockey

7. the trainer

8. the weight it carries

9. the post position

10. the horse's final time ability

11. racing luck

12. **the current condition of the horse**

The Horse's Particular Running Style

A horse's running style can usually be designated by one of four general categories:

- Frontrunner (F)

- Presser/Frontrunner (P/F)

- Presser (P)

- Closer (C)

These designations give a good indication of where the horse likes to position itself in relation to the herd. Horses that must have the lead in order to win are severely compromised when confronted with other frontrunners with better pace numbers. These "outrun speed" types are almost sure to falter when they cannot "get to the top". If you happen to notice these outrun frontrunners hanging on for second or third, it may be indicative of a speed bias.

The presser/frontrunner is a horse that can contest or take the lead if it chooses, but typically is found rating a length or two off the early fractions. These horses are strong contenders if both their pace and final numbers stack up. Presser/frontrunners can usually be counted upon to make their presence felt at some point during the race, and their versatile running style allows them to adapt to different pace scenarios more successfully than the one dimensional frontrunners.

Pressers normally like to lay two to four lengths off the lead and make a move on the turn to reach striking position. They do not possess quite the tactical speed or front-running ability of presser/ frontrunners, and thus may have a tougher time if facing "lone speed" or a slower than normal pace.

Closers usually take the worst of it on the dirt (turf is quite a different matter). Having little or no early speed, they are usually found lagging near the back of the pack, dependent upon an honest pace and a good trip to get the job done. They may be exciting to watch roaring down the stretch, but are notoriously poor betting propositions unless a hotly contested pace or a strong anti-speed bias is operative.

The Pace Demands of the Race

Once we have determined the likely positional tendencies of the entrants, we can now look at the specific pace configuration or match-up. Positional speed tendencies and pace numbers are related but not the same by any means. A presser who runs 80 pace numbers will probably not be head-and-head with a frontrunner who also runs 80 pace numbers. As detailed earlier, most horses develop certain "herd" tendencies, and it is not as easy as one might think for a trainer or jockey to engineer a dramatic reversal in style. While a frontrunner almost always tries for the lead, a presser is usually content to lay a bit off the pace even if it has pace numbers as good as the frontrunner. If a smart barn or jockey realizes they can seize the lead with a presser, they may go for it, but the idea to remember is that positional tendencies and pace numbers are not interchangeable. They must be evaluated and incorporated into a comprehensive analysis.

Any frontrunner with a two point pace advantage (remember the **pace number** is always in parentheses and represents four furlong velocity) is a threat to wire the field if his final numbers are competitive and he is in good condition. If a speed bias exists, a lone frontrunner becomes dangerous even if its final numbers are weaker than the other main contenders. Its early advantage will prove more powerful due to the prevailing bias. On extremely speed-biased tracks, the **two furlong number** (to the right of the pace number in dirt sprints) should be given a careful look. Normally, I don't give the 2f number much consideration (as most horses can run pretty fast for a quarter mile), but when these big speed biases occur, it is worth your attention. The early advantage is now a powerful edge, and on days like these, I have been known to throw the final numbers out the window and focus on the 2f and 4f numbers.

The situation becomes more complex when there is a mix of running styles in the race. If there are multiple F's, and one has a significant pace advantage (2 points or more), it may put away the other F's with minimal resistance and hold off the pressers and closers. However, when there are multiple F's, and none of them has a pace number edge, a pace battle is very likely. P/F's and P's are the most likely beneficiaries in this scenario. When there are four or more F's, a pace meltdown is almost assured, and even the P/F's may join the fray too early, setting it up for P's and C's.

In races with no confirmed frontrunners, give the edge to P/F's and P's with solid pace numbers, all else being equal.

For most handicappers, one of the toughest races to analyze is one in which none of the entrants has shown the recent willingness or ability to be on or near the lead in the early stages. This is where a skilled reinsman who knows how to read the *Racing Form* (or a shrewd trainer armed with **EQUIFORM** pace numbers) can attempt to "steal" the race, especially if the horse draws a favorable post. The drawback to this ploy is that many horses will not respond when asked to deviate from their customary running style. That is why a top rider can make all the difference in these situations.

Distance

If I have learned one universal truth concerning dirt racing, it is that unchallenged early speed wins over any distance and any surface. If a frontrunner is allowed to set comfortable (for itself) early splits and effectively ration its reserves of energy, it will usually defeat horses of equal final time ability and, often, have enough left to withstand the late efforts of superior final figure horses. Don't be reluctant to bet these speed types stretching out if they have the requisite pace advantage, acceptable breeding for the distance, and are within a point or two on final time. You will be well rewarded. Also, as you will see later, by looking at the relative distribution of the Equiform pace and final numbers, we can determine which horses display the best patterns to stretch out successfully.

As Equiform provides six-furlong numbers for all dirt races longer than three-quarters of a mile, we can snare some nice overlays on horses turning back in distance. Compare the **turnback number** (to the left of the pace number) against the final sprint (or turnback numbers) of the other contenders, and you will sometimes land on a real live long shot. Often, these turnback horses are concealed from the public and "sheet" players who focus on final time figures. If a horse fades severely in a race longer than six furlongs, its final number may look poor, but it may actually have run well for the first three-quarters. The one caveat I suggest in this situation regards positional analysis. A frontrunner or presser/frontrunner in routes may have a difficult time getting the lead in sprints, so make sure it has not only a good turnback number, but also the pace numbers and conditioning to be competitive.

On a final note concerning distance, we do believe that certain horses prefer certain distances. Some animals can handle a variety of distances effectively, but many have distinct preferences. I don't know if they still subscribe to the theory, but I remember attending a "sheets" seminar many moons ago, where they claimed 80% of horses could produce the same figures between 6f and 1-1/8 miles. We disagree. Uncovering these subtle preferences can help you make the right decision among a few apparently evenly matched contenders.

Surface

Our off track symbols should help you determine a horse's previous ability to handle different types of "off" surfaces. For horses that have never run on off tracks, there are several reputable sources that publish pedigree ratings for this purpose. However, once the animals have encountered off tracks a couple of times, we suggest you use actual races to evaluate their off-track ability. Also, keep in mind that a horse may run differently in the slop at Aqueduct than it does at the Fair Grounds. Due to soil composition and other elements, all off tracks are not the same.

The same rules apply to turf racing. We will use breeding guides, pedigree, and turf ratings for horses with 0-2 starts on the grass, but will then rely on actual grass performance.

On both off tracks and turf, do not make the same mistake most of your competition does when assessing a horse's ability on these surfaces. Often, I have heard a player say that a particular horse doesn't like mud/turf because its overall box score reads something like 37 10-6-4, but 10 1-1-2 on wet tracks. This may or may not be true. Maybe the horse happened to catch some of the better fields it's faced on those off-track days. What's really important are the numbers it ran on off tracks or turf, not if it won or came in the money. We are measuring *performance*, not *wins and losses*.

As we are on the subject of surface, now is a good time to expound on the fundamental difference between dirt and turf racing. Most dirt racing in North America, especially sprints, revolves around early position/speed and deceleration. Horses go as fast as they can for as far as they can while trying to take the shortest route home.

Turf racing involves a whole different set of dynamics. While positional/tactical speed is an advantage on the dirt, finishing ability is the prime ingredient for success on the weeds. Lone frontrunners are still playable on the grass, but make sure they have proven grass ability (or the appropriate turf breeding if lightly raced). We have no qualms about backing lightly raced animals with excellent turf pedigrees, but are reluctant to back more seasoned horses trying turf for the first time against grass veterans. First of all, if the horse had real turf ability, a capable trainer would probably have tried it on the surface earlier in its career. Secondly, the horse may not adapt to the tighter turns, the jostling for position, and the furious finishes that are characteristic of racing on the green.

I have commented for about a decade that the turf figures of most major speed figure services are askew. At least Andy Beyer was man enough to admit in a *Racing Form* article a few years back that his turf figures were flawed, and he was making an effort to improve them. Back in the '80s, when I was a "sheets" player, I had a few discussions with the Lens (Ragozin and Freidman) regarding their turf figures. My main thrust was why didn't top grass horses like Manila or Pebbles or

Miesque (or more recently Lure) run as good numbers as top dirt horses. Alysheba and Easy Goer could hit 0's but the big grass horses got 2's or 3's (on their scale, the lower the figure, the better the performance). Their answers were rather vague and unconvincing.

It seemed to me that a truly championship quality grass horse should produce numbers as good as its dirt counterpart. In every crop in North America (which number around 35,000 these days), you have a better chance of getting a Kentucky Derby winner than an Epsom Derby winner. Most horses here are bred for speed, not going long on the grass at classic distances. Therefore, the odds of producing a superior dirt animal are greater than producing a classic distance, turf horse. However, at the highest echelons, greatness is greatness. Does anyone really think Secretariat wasn't as good on the grass as he was on the dirt? In his first grass attempt, he went to the top and demolished turf champion Tentam in a hand ride.

Another factor to consider is that grass racing tends to be more competitive than dirt racing. As a smaller segment of the overall population participates (many tracks still don't even have turf racing), grass races usually draw large fields. Also, since grass horses usually distribute most of their energy late in the race, the finishes are much closer. It is quite common to see a dirt horse drawing off to win by six or eight lengths or even more. You will rarely see this on the grass because the early segments of most grass races are an exercise in rating and position, which means the horses only have a half-mile or so to demonstrate their real ability. The clustered finishes that characterize turf racing make closing ability paramount. At 1-1/4 miles on the Belmont inner turf, I have witnessed high-priced claiming horses negotiate the final quarter mile in 22 and change. Tell me the last time you saw that in a dirt race at ten furlongs! The real point is that turf racing is an entirely different ballgame. To analyze these races effectively, a unique paradigm, which will be detailed later, is required.

The success we have enjoyed betting surface switches over the last several years has only strengthened our opinion that the dirt/turf relationships of some prominent figure makers are awry. Our research indicates that the turf numbers of these services are a touch slow when compared to their dirt numbers. The discrepancy is relatively hidden when all the horses have been regularly competing on the grass, as everyone's grass figure is slower, but the relative relationship is constant. However, when turf horses go to the dirt or vice versa, the relationship is erratic.

We believe the relationship between our dirt and turf numbers is more accurate, and have scores of juicy mutuel prices to illustrate the point. The prime situations in which to take advantage of the above discrepancy are when a horse is racing on the dirt for the first time after a grass race(s) or going back to the dirt after a few turf races. The turf numbers on The Xtras will usually be relatively higher (faster) than the corresponding turf numbers of other services. If the horse is lightly raced, and not particularly bred for grass, it should be able to replicate or even improve upon its Equiform grass number(s). It will be underbet by the crowd, as the turf numbers of other services won't look as good. With horses switching back to the dirt, the price differential will probably not be as great, as the horse has back dirt figures that all players can evaluate. However, even in this situation, the recent Equiform grass numbers may signal an improved effort at overlaid odds.

Remember, a turf race is denoted by an equal sign (=) before the final number and after the pace number. All off-track/off-turf symbols appear to the left of the final number.

Bias

Although several well-known figure makers pay scant attention to track bias, and some even dismiss it entirely, we staunchly believe it exists. Having said that, we also believe that accurately identifying a bias is often a formidable task that requires considerable handicapping skills.

Several factors impact on the bias of a given track at any particular moment – soil composition, soil depth, moisture, rain, sun, wind, and the "configuration" of the racing oval itself, to name a few. All else being equal, tracks with tight turns like Saratoga and the Aqueduct inner dirt favor speed, whereas Belmont Park, with its sweeping turns, tends to be more hospitable to off the pace types.

How many times have you been at the track when a couple of speed-balls, breaking from inside posts, win the first two races? All of the wise guys nod toward each other, confident the track is favoring inside speed. Unfortunately for them, this is not always the case. These two horses may have been lone frontrunners in their respective races and could have wired their fields from any post over just about any surface.

Players who hastily formulate bias opinions without the requisite analysis will be confounded when horses with different running styles capture races later on the card. Another curve occurs when the bias changes during the day or when the route bias (usually a two-turn race) is different than the sprint bias.

The strongest clue that a bias exists occurs when one sees a horse do something out of the ordinary. A faint-hearted sprinter, who habitually squanders leads in the stretch, posts some decent fractions, repels a couple of challenges and draws out to a victory. Several possibilities exist to explain this result.

1. a weaker than average field for the class

2. a type of change

    (a) jockey

    (b) trainer

    (c) equipment (blinkers, mud caulks, bar shoe off, etc)

    (d) training methods (layoff, surface switch, stretch-out, etc)

3. a strong pace advantage

4. a change in medication (lasix, bute, etc)

5. illegal drugs

6. bias

Only after evaluating all of the above factors and their interrelationship would we conclude a bias might exist. Later races would be used to either confirm or dispel the theory.

In conjunction with bias, I would like to again mention *ground loss*. One of the difficulties I encountered in using "sheet" numbers was their lack of bias consideration. I usually had to make "adjustments to their ground loss adjustments" as previous biases skewed their figures and subsequent pattern analysis. Consider a speed horse, that battles for the lead into deep stretch on a dead rail, losing by a length. This horse would get a significantly poorer figure than a horse that swung wide on the turn and rolled home on the *good* footing out in the middle of the track. This just does not make sense. Who really ran the better race or expended more energy?

Since The Xtras are a superior product for evaluating condition, we are able to explain some apparently aberrant performances that cause others to make poor judgments regarding bias.

Another variable to consider in evaluating bias is statistical randomness. On some days, speed horses may win most of the races, not because of any inherent conditioning edge *or* because of a bias, but by pure chance. Although we firmly attest to the influence of biases, we also feel that often what others view as bias is simply random noise.

In summary, correctly identifying biases is one of the most problematical yet rewarding pieces of the handicapping puzzle. Incorporating previous biases into your analysis will help you understand current condition. However, the biggest edge accrues to those who can detect a bias in the early races before the crowd catches on. This uncommon ability can lead to some dramatically profitable results, especially utilizing The Xtras.

The Jockey

The jockey factor is probably the most overrated variable in thoroughbred racing. Jerry Bailey, Gary Stevens, Pat Day and other top riders are obviously better than most, but are so overbet by an adoring public, that a flat bet on all of their mounts at a given meeting usually leads to greater percentage losses than the track take.

For example, midway through the 1999 Belmont spring meet, Bailey had 22 wins from 84 mounts at an average mutuel of $5.89. It doesn't take a rocket scientist to figure out that this leads to a negative twenty-three percent return on investment. We all know that Bailey is one the best jockeys in the world but, for pari-mutuel purposes, he is a major price depressant.

Meanwhile, at the same Belmont meet, Robbie Davis was 16 for 87 at an average price of $14.32. Jean-Luc Samyn was 7 for 46 at an average of $24.99. Those kinds of numbers spell profits. Speaking of Samyn, although "Samyn on the green" may be poetically pleasing to New Yorkers, the data isn't as conclusive. In several years over the last decade, Samyn has shown a better return on investment on the dirt than on the green stuff. Beware of conventional racetrack wisdom – it is often misguided.

What many race-goers fail to recognize is that if an animal is not in condition, a top jockey isn't going to make much of a difference. Refrigerator Perry might have been able to win the '73 Belmont aboard Secretariat, and Jerry Bailey can't win if the horse he's on isn't in condition or realistically placed. As much as Bailey is overbet in New York (especially when riding for Bill Mott), nobody is more overplayed than Pat Day in Kentucky. "Pat Day is hot", "Patty is due to win one", or "Day is a bum" can be heard echoing through the grandstand. What do people expect when they back a legitimate 10/1 shot down to 4/1 simply because Day is named to ride? One could probably make a decent living by just betting against false Day favorites.

You gotta get the horses. Top jockeys become top jockeys due to a combination of physical riding ability, superior judgment, and good agents. The agent factor should not be underestimated. A perceptive agent with good handicapping skills and a flair for salesmanship can make a star out of a merely competent rider. Of course, as a jockey journeys to the top, he gets better mounts, which leads to more winning and even choicer riding assignments. This process creates a wonderful loop at the apex of the riding pyramid, but also makes it quite difficult for some very good riders without the proper connections to crack into the elite circle. Sometimes a new face will burst onto the scene (Steve Cauthen) or an older one will finally arrive on the national stage (Jorge Chavez), but usually, it is the same old crew atop the standings.

A jockey cannot make a horse more racing fit than it already is when it arrives in the paddock. He may be able to calm a nervous animal, but he is basically at the mercy of the trainer to have the horse healthy and ready for the task at hand. The edge in employing a top jockey is that they make fewer mistakes. They are less likely to get into trouble, misjudge the pace, or stay on the inside when the rail is obviously dead, etc. Other than their superior judgment, there is not a whole lot of difference between the top riders and other competent journeymen at any particular meet. What is different is the public's *perception* of their respective abilities. Put a capable journeyman on the best horse, and he will win almost as often as a top five rider, but at much more appealing prices. The times he loses due to a poor ride when a Bailey would have won is more than compensated for in price. Believe me when I tell you, I have made much more money betting the likes of Richard Migliore, Filiberto Leon, Shaun Bridgmohan, and until recently John Velazquez, than I have betting Mike Smith or Jerry Bailey.

The Trainer

While the jockey factor tends to be overbet, the trainer factor is often underrated. No individual has more influence over a horse's performance than does the trainer. True, big name trainers are often overbet like their riding counterparts, but top trainers exert a significantly greater impact on race outcomes than top riders. A highly skilled jockey can only move a horse up so much, but an equally adroit trainer can literally work wonders.

Only a Hall-of-Famer like Allen Jerkens could take a confirmed sprinter like Autoroute, give him a series of mile workouts, and send him out to set a track record going two turns on the Aqueduct inner track. I have seen Bill Mott handle a young grass horse (Tangazi, for example) so cleverly, that the horse doesn't take more than a one point backward move for its first ten or twelve races. Although he has now departed to the big winners' circle in the sky, the legendary Charlie Whittingham was a master at pointing a horse for a specific engagement. After capturing the 1986 Arlington Million with Allen Paulson's

Estrapade, the Bald Eagle was asked when he thought he had the race won. "When I entered her," Whittingham replied.

As proficient as top trainers are, the poor ones are equally inept. Whether it is a paucity of decent racing stock, ill-conceived training methods, inappropriate placement, or a host of other possibilities, bad trainers, by definition, rarely win. The few occasions I might back these low percentage types are in cheaper races, where most of the field is in the hands of equally inferior conditioners. If two animals with roughly equal ability are about the same price, almost always give the edge to the better trainer.

Just as capable journeymen who are not household names can provide good value, so do competent low-key trainers. One of my favorite angles along these lines would be a trainer whose record at the current meeting reads something like (4 0-2-1). Who knows, with a little bit of racing luck the guy may have had two wins. With only four starters, the public probably won't have a good feel for this particular trainer. Low-key barns go on hot streaks just like the big boys, but at much better prices.

Volumes have been written on trainer moves, angles, and patterns. Trainer statistics are available from a variety of sources, covering everything from first-time starters to one-year layoffs. A lot of these statistics are unimportant if not related to what the barn is doing *now*. Who really cares that out of 1432 starters over the last five years, trainer A wins at 19% for a return of $1.96 per $2.00? What has he done over the last year - the last three months - the last month - the last ten days? Current trends should normally take precedence over long term data.

Get to know the strengths and weaknesses of the top twenty or thirty trainers on your circuit (they probably win 80% of the races). Don't rely on computer printouts with 70 or 80 categories of trainer stats. Although there may be a few nuggets in the mountain of data, you may get left at the pass. Probably the best way for tracking trainers is the method suggested by Dave Litfin, New York handicapper for the *Daily Racing Form*. Litfin recommends clipping the past performances of all a trainer's horses for the last few months and entering them in a notebook. It takes some effort, but you will begin to reap dividends sooner than you think. You might notice a trainer winning only for a certain owner, a unique workout pattern, a claiming angle, a layoff pattern, etc.

Shrewd trainers are not averse to cashing a bet now and then. A few are also aware that equally shrewd handicappers follow their every move. All of a sudden, a trainer who is 1 for 53 with first-time starters clicks with his next two debuters at nice prices. The long-term stats say he is now 3 for 53 with first-time starters, not an inspiring record. But, I would give this guy's next first-timer a careful evaluation. See what I mean about statistics?

In summary, by bringing a degree of discrimination to the analysis of trainer patterns and recognizing the subtleties in the data, you will be furlongs ahead of the competition.

Weight

Weight is factored into all Equiform numbers. Each five pounds of weight is equivalent to one point. The length value of a point varies according to distance. As mentioned earlier, one point is about one length at four furlongs, 1-1/2 lengths at six furlongs, 2 lengths at a mile, and 2-1/2 lengths at ten furlongs.

Weight is already included in the numbers the horse has previously earned. But when analyzing an upcoming race, you must incorporate the assigned weight into your calculations. For example, if you think two horses rate to run 73's, but one is carrying 118 pounds and the other 112 pounds, the 112 horse has a little more than a point edge, all else being equal.

The method I use to simplify the weight adjustment process is to use 115 as a baseline weight. Then, I adjust the numbers I expect the horses to run by 1/5 point (0.20) for each pound they are assigned above or below this benchmark. To illustrate – I expect Horse A to run a 68, Horse B a 69, and Horse C a 67.5. Their respective assigned weights are 112, 121, and 114. After making the recommended adjustments, my final projections would be 68.6 for Horse A, 67.8 for Horse B, and 67.7 for Horse C.

Although the five pounds = one point formula is accurate for the majority of the thoroughbred population, there are certain anomalies. Due to conformation, bone structure, lung capacity and other variables, some horses can handle higher weights better than most. An 800-pound, two-year-old filly can hardly be expected to carry 137 pounds as efficiently as handicap luminaries such as Forego or Dr. Fager.

For practical purposes, however, our weight adjustments are quite accurate and should be factored into your analysis.

Post Position

Post position analysis can be an integral part of the handicapping process at certain distances at particular tracks. However, as will be elaborated upon later, the manner in which most current post position statistics are presented can be misleading.

There is no question that all else being equal, horses with inside posts going two turns (or three, for that matter), with a relatively short run to the first turn, have a decided advantage over horses breaking from the outside. Obviously, this advantage becomes greater on good rail days, and even more so when horses on the inside are F's (frontrunners) or P/F's (presser/frontrunners). The ability to establish good position with minimal effort pays dividends in the later stages. To downgrade (as some figure makers do) the performances of horses with tactical speed, who are able to consistently save ground, is courting inaccuracy. Closers who draw outside posts are not as compromised as speed horses. Closers can often manage to tuck in somewhere near the rail and save ground on the first turn, as they are not intent on being close to the early pace.

As mentioned earlier, horses that can get over to the rail and hold their position have less distance to cover than horses that traverse the outside paths. However, this edge can be neutralized or even become a liability on days where the rail and/or other inside paths are dead, especially when lazy or incompetent riders are not aware of the situation.

As for one turn races, the same factors are at play, but usually, the advantage is not as pronounced. In fact, at certain tracks, outside

Winning Posts, Belmont Park, May 12 – June 24, 1999
Main Track Sprints

PP	STARTS	WINS	WIN PCT
1	128	15	12
2	128	15	12
3	128	17	13
4	128	19	15
5	126	16	13
6	118	18	15
7	98	10	10
8	68	6	9
9	40	8	20
10	21	3	14
11	11	1	9
12	5	0	0

posts do very well in races at seven furlongs to a mile out of a chute (Aqueduct and Belmont, in particular). This phenomenon can be due to several factors. Often, horses on the inside shy away or toward the gap in the chute where no railing is present. Also, with an elongated run to the first turn, the riders of horses posted outside do not have to push their mounts as hard for early position. They get a better view of how the race is shaping up in front of them, have less traffic to worry about, and can often secure a position on the "crown" of the track. Long-time New York players remember Ussery's alley, where Bobby Ussery, when breaking from an outside post would steer his mounts so wide on the backstretch that they would disappear from the television pan shot, only to begin that inexorable swoop down the slope nearing the turn. Ussery felt that the minimal ground he lost was more than made up for by the momentum his horse gathered entering the turn. We agree, although it takes a very skilled rider to turn the trick.

   The difficulty in interpreting most published post position statistics (like the ones in the *Daily Racing Form*) is that the data for different sprint and route distances are combined into just two categories – sprints and routes. A more accurate method would be to group the data according to specific distances (a beneficial post at six furlongs could be a poor post at seven furlongs). A second major flaw is that by presenting the data by winning percentage per post, someone without a knack for numbers could draw a false conclusion. Take a look at the table of Winning Posts from the first six weeks of the 1999 Belmont spring meet (page 46).

Often, one will see racing writers and analysts mention that the inside posts at a particular track are winning at 14%, while outside posts are winning at only 8%. In isolation, this is a meaningless or even misleading observation. After all, there are at least 12 horses in the race if there is a horse in the 12 post. So all else being equal, horses from the 12 post should win 1/12 of the races or about 8%.

To illustrate this point more clearly, let's break down the above post position data. We can infer the following regarding the field sizes of the sprint races.

2	races with	4	horses
8	races with	5	horses
20	races with	6	horses
30	races with	7	horses
28	races with	8	horses
19	races with	9	horses
10	races with	10	horses
6	races with	11	horses
5	races with	12	horses

Horses breaking from the four inside posts competed in 30 races of six horses or less. Their natural probabilities of winning these races ranged from 25% in a four-horse field to 16.7% in a six-horse field. A horse breaking from the 12 post has at best a natural probability of 8.3% (there could be more than 12 horses). To group these completely different situations into a simple winning percentage chart isn't very illuminating.

To compound matters further, sample sizes are often small. A couple of photo finishes could make a post look better or worse than it really is. Finally, a certain post (like the 9 post in our Belmont example) may be doing well because a few odds-on horses just happened to get the 9 pill in the post position draw.

In summary, rushing to judgments regarding the effects of post positions can lead to serious misconceptions. Long-term trends (a few years, assuming no radical changes in track configuration, surface or run-ups), should take precedence over short-term sampling. However, be on the lookout for current trends due to weather, bias, track condition, and other factors.

Final Time Ability

Twenty or thirty years ago, astute handicappers with access to good variant-adjusted final time figures could generate substantial profits. After all, faster horses should beat slower horses, and at that time, the faster horses were often concealed from a public weaned on raw final time and class handicapping. However, as more good figures became available, it became necessary to understand patterns in the figures to retain an edge.

When I first started using the "sheets" in the 1980s, terms like "bounce" and "top" were used and understood by only a small fraternity of players. Now, we see these terms bandied about in the general racing press. As in all markets, when any information becomes public knowledge, its usefulness for making excess returns diminishes or evaporates.

Even today, however, knowing which horses in a race have run the best final time figures in the past assists one in predicting how fast they might perform in the future.

I have found final time pattern analysis to be most useful in races for older horses (four-year-olds and up) competing in mid-priced claimers all the way up to stakes races. Older animals have usually established certain parameters of ability and have been exposed to varying pace scenarios, off tracks, and different distances. They are unlikely to make a new four-point final top or run a pace number ten points faster than normal. An overview of the pace match-up is still useful, but is not as critical as when dealing with maiden claimers, maiden specials, or straight claiming and allowance races for younger, developing horses.

If a horse consistently runs relatively fast final numbers, he is by all means a serious contender. Unfortunately, these types of reliable older performers tend to be overbet by the crowd. A better strategy is to look for horses that are cycling or edging back toward a big effort. These animals are not so easy to isolate and provide better returns.

In my own betting, I proceed with caution when handicapping bottom of the barrel, straight claiming races on any circuit. The horses entered in these races are often unsound and/or inconsistent. Trainers are known to "experiment" quite frequently at these lower echelons, and form cycle analysis is often not the key. It amazes me how a $5,000 claimer can be bet down to 3/5. I can understand how Cigar can be 3/5, but cheap claimers are hardly ever worth that kind of risk.

I am not a subscriber to the theory of "class" handicapping, with one exception. In Grade I and Grade II races, I do believe horses that have won or been competitive at these levels previously should be given an edge, all else being equal.

My definition of class is one word – *Secretariat*!

The ability to accelerate and seize command of a race at any time is what class is all about. Very few animals, regardless of relative class level, demonstrate this ability. To possess this characteristic at the pinnacle of the sport is the hallmark of a champion.

For those of you who don't remember, Secretariat set a track record in each leg of the 1973 Triple Crown. In the Kentucky Derby, he broke the two-minute barrier established by Northern Dancer, running each successive quarter-mile faster than the previous one. In the Preakness, when other riders tried to slow down the pace, jockey Ron Turcotte sent Secretariat from last to first on the clubhouse turn in an astonishing display of raw speed and agility. Then in the Belmont, he scorched the first six furlongs in 1:09.4 en route to an unheard of 2:24 for the mile and a half. All three classics were won in a different manner, with the only constant being Secretariat's ability to turn on the after burners whenever he pleased.

I have seen some great ones in my time. Kelso, Damascus, Buckpasser, Dr. Fager, Affirmed, Ruffian, Seattle Slew, Forego, Pebbles, Spectacular Bid, Personal Ensign, Sunday Silence, Easy Goer, Alysheba,

Miesque, Cigar – champions, one and all. But none of them could beat you in as many ways as Big Red.

In my mind, the answer will always be Secretariat.

Racing Luck

We believe in the adage that luck is the residue of design. This is usually true over the long haul but, in the near term, the goddess of racing can precipitate many unforeseen outcomes.

For example, in a race with three F's (frontrunners), two could get caught in a tangle out of the gate. This leaves the other F horse loose on the lead, and you can throw your pace analysis out the window. A horse could be in great condition only to receive the proverbial "ride from hell". Another horse could fall right in front of your horse. A horse could get doused with a can of beer (Bombay Duck in the Kentucky Derby) – jump a shadow (Dayjur in the Breeders' Cup) – get steadied three times inside the eighth pole (Laurent Goosens up) – have its rider misjudge the finish line (Willie Shoemaker on Gallant Man in the Derby) – or have a rider who knows where the finish line is, but forgets that in a two-mile race on the Aqueduct inner track, you must pass it twice (Jorge Chavez when he first came to New York).

At times, horses have to deal with a fan trying to punch out its rider (Artax with Chavez aboard on the '99 Preakness under card), a flock of geese on the turf course, assistant starters who don't promptly release their tails at the break, and other horses trying to savage them.

We all have our favorite horror stories but, over time, things usually even out. It has always amused me that when a handicapper wins a photo it seems preordained. After all, he *did* pick the winner. But when this same handicapper loses a photo, it's a bad beat. How come most players don't feel that winning by a nose is lucky? One of the keys to successful wagering is to not get too elated when things are going well nor too despondent when you lose a few photos. How we handle both winning and losing reveals a lot about ourselves. "Bad beats" shouldn't bother you too much. Bad bets should. If you bet on a 10/1 shot that loses by a nose, you probably made a good play, as the horse ran better than expected. If out of frustration, sentiment or sheer compulsion, you bet a horse at 2/1 just for some "action", you are asking for trouble.

Nurturing the discipline to make only good bets is not easy. We all like to see our opinions validated as frequently as possible, even if it means betting on a 9/5 shot that offers no value. But to win in the end, we must receive better than fair value for our wagering dollar. We don't keep score by how many winners we pick, but by how much money we win. Anybody can be tough when things are going good, but knowing how to handle losing streaks is what separates professionals from casual players. If you gamble frequently, you are going to have losing streaks. Anybody who plays every day and denies this is kin to Pinocchio.

Try to stay on an even keel. Even if you are a weekend warrior, resist the temptation to try and "get out" in the last race unless something really looks appealing. The next weekend will be here before you know it.

Through stewards' capricious disqualifications, the holes on the hedge that never materialize, the "stiff" jobs and your own mistakes, maintain your composure. It is all part of the game, and if you allow these imponderables to upset your equilibrium, a sudden depletion in your bankroll will almost surely follow.

Condition

Although the above eleven variables play a role in race outcomes, all of them taken together are not as important as the horse's current form or **condition**. If a horse is not physically in shape to run a competitive race, all the sophisticated analysis in the world isn't going to land him in the winners' circle.

Through a concerted effort, one can learn to be a better judge of an animal's physical appearance in the paddock and post parade. It is not a skill that is easily acquired. I like to see an alert animal, with an arched neck, ears pricked and a nicely dappled coat as much as the next person, but if the horse doesn't have the ability to be competitive, all the good looks don't really amount to much. However, if you are torn between two 4/1 shots in a five-horse field, and one of them starts acting up in the paddock, breaking out in a lather, your course of action seems clear. Even here, however, knowing the behavioral tendencies of the specific horse could alter the outlook. Manila, the 1986 Breeders Cup turf champion, would often break out in the post parade without it visibly affecting his performance.

The trainer has a major impact on a horse's current condition. With a regimen of workouts and/or prep races, good trainers handle their charges carefully, spotting them where they have a realistic chance to get the money. Good feed, nutritional supplements, equipment, and legal medications are used in the hope of maximizing the animal's inherent capabilities. If the trainer brings a fit and happy horse to the paddock, his mission is accomplished. It is now up to the handicapper to assess the horse's probable performance in relation to the competition and determine fair odds.

Although our pace and final numbers play the most integral role in evaluating likely performance, players should bring all the knowledge they have to the table. If a horse looks like good value on paper, but his trainer is mired in an 0/30 drought, you should probably demand better odds than if the trainer is four for his last ten. If the skies open up six minutes to post, a breeding analysis for wet track ability is in order. A late scratch could affect the pace scenario, a major contender could act up in the post parade, bar shoes off could be announced a few minutes before pick six betting closes, etc. Still, with all the uncertainties that confront the bettor, he should rely on form cycle and condition analysis as the cornerstone of his approach.

Horses can react in one of three basic ways from race to race:

1. stay at roughly the same level

2. move forward

3. regress

If the handicapper can predict the likelihood of these three possible outcomes significantly better than the public, he is on the road to profitability. A major flaw in many players' view of the game is thinking in a linear fashion. Horse X beat Horse Y the last two times they met, so why shouldn't X beat Y today? If you think like this, it is time for a change. Start thinking cyclically. Only a few performers at any class level are able to exhibit steady development early in their careers and then, having reached maturity as four or five year-olds, maintain a consistent level of performance. Older geldings, especially grass horses, typify this kind of animal. The race to race performance of most horses, especially fillies, can vary erratically. Try not to look for history to repeat itself – it usually doesn't. Instead, envision each previous race as part of a constantly evolving process of improvement and decline.

In the rest of this book, we will explain how to use our data effectively. Several concepts and methods will be introduced and illustrated. Our goal is to assist the handicapper in interpreting the information on The Xtras to make superior judgments regarding a horse's current condition and potential.

With a sincere effort from the reader, we are confident that both your understanding of the game and your bottom line will improve considerably.

Part II

Blinkers Off

Exploring THE XTRAS

Chapter 7

The New Pace Top

Lifetime

Let's say it one more time: **Condition** is the paramount handicapping factor. Class, pace, distance, final-time ability and all other factors are relevant of course, but they must all be evaluated in relation to the horse's current condition. A player who is able to assess this variable significantly better than the competition will have a decisive edge at the windows. **THE XTRAS** are the single most effective tool for predicting a horse's current condition.

Most dirt races in North America, especially sprints, are exercises in *deceleration*. Absent a dead rail or anti-speed bias, horses that are able to break alertly and establish prominent early position enjoy a tactical advantage. These early leaders and pressers can often save ground near the inside and avoid traffic problems in the latter stages of the race.

As the initial portions of dirt races are usually run the quickest, a horse that exhibits improved early speed is usually showing signs of development. Young horses with gradually improving pace and final numbers are always worth a second look. Remember, however, that if the final number move is too large, a regression (bounce) will occur sooner or later - usually sooner, if you have gotten careless and made an ill-advised wager. Smaller, incremental moves, particularly in the final number, are more likely to produce another immediate peak effort.

Of all the discoveries **EQUIFORM's** research has unearthed, one of the most powerful is also one of the easiest to spot – the **new pace top**. You will see this pattern several times a day no matter what track(s) you play. The pace number, which measures four furlong velocity at all distances, is in parentheses just to the right of the final and turnback number grid. If the final number that resulted from the new pace top (NPT) was not a significant top (two points or more), an improvement in the final number is quite likely next time out.

The most valuable use of this elementary pattern occurs when the horse runs an "off" final number when running the new pace top. The public will generally be a little perplexed about the animal's current condition and will be unsure what to expect next. But based on years of research, Equiform can predict that approximately 70% of the time the horse will make a nice forward move. This is true because a horse has only so much energy to distribute during a race. If it exerts itself more than normal in the early portion, its final time usually suffers. However, the improved early pace in the most stressful segment of the race usually portends better days down the road.

On pages 61−64, you will find The Xtras for some horses as they appeared on race-day.[1] All of them had run a new pace top in their last race, along with a final number below their previous best. The public and most other figure players are often oblivious to this strong pattern. Consequently, they cannot predict a forward move with any degree of confidence. This translates into good wagering value for users of The Xtras.

All of these horses won their next starts. From favorites to long shots, from youngsters to old veterans, and from maiden claimers to Grade I stake races, the new pace top performs its magic. Of course, horses naturally record higher numbers as they gain more seasoning, with second and third time starters often exhibiting extreme volatility. However, predicting the timing of these swings is another matter, and users of The Xtras have the information to anticipate these moves more precisely. Below are the final numbers these horses earned in their next start after the new pace top, along with the win prices.

---

[1]For ease of presentation, some examples of The Xtras have been reformatted. All the numbers appear, but some date spacing has been condensed.

Ordained	75"	$ 6.20
Balto Star	71-	$28.20
Darling Deputy	73	$ 7.60
Fighting Spirit	68-	$13.40
Mr Lion Heart	68-	$36.80
Chase A Star	69-	$28.60
Millennium Wind	80-	$10.20
Icicle Angel	71+	$41.60

On February 17, 2001, at Gulfstream Park, The Fountain of Youth Stakes, an early Kentucky Derby prep, was contested over 1-1/16 miles. Take a look at the major contenders for that race as they appeared on The Xtras on pages 65-67.

The race was quite competitive. The deserving favorite, Outofthebox, who had run a 74" and a 76 in routes as a two-year old, came back right in line with a 74" in January, and had Jerry Bailey at the helm. There were several other interesting possibilities. Buckle Down Ben was coming off a new pace top, earning a final number just off his two-year old top. City Zip had danced all the dances as a 2yo, and had come back with a strong sprint prep to open the year, but he had the look of an early bloomer, who might not relish the longer distances. Global Gait had done nothing wrong in his 2yo campaign (note the NPT in late November), and was now under the tutelage of Bob Baffert. Meetyouathebrig and Holiday Thunder also had some good 2yo form, and both were making their 2001 debut. All the others, save one, looked too slow to threaten.

Songandaprayer, owned in part by former Duke basketball star Bobby Hurley, had a very nice look. After breaking his maiden at Monmouth Park with a 70" in June 2000, he was laid off for five months, but returned with a 76- in the fog at Aqueduct. In the Holy Bull Stakes, his first time around two turns, he flashed blazing early speed, running an (88) NPT in the process. With that big 2yo number buttressing the NPT, Songandaprayer had every right to be considered a serious contender. In addition, he had a top rider in Edgar Prado, and figured to get the lead on the usually speed-favoring Gulfstream strip.

Having studied the race, it was now time to decide if there was a wager worth making. In a field this contentious and with lots of question marks concerning the layoff horses, Outofthebox just wasn't enough price at 5/2. But Songandaprayer at 18/1 was an outstanding play. I made his real odds in the 6/1 to 8/1 range. Prado got him to the front, and the ever-prescient Bailey, sensing a theft, sent Outofthebox after him on the far turn, but Songandaprayer dug in and drew off to a $38.00 mutuel.

The seventh race at Aqueduct on January 26, 2001 was a bonanza for Equiform players. Both John Paul Too and Pure Harmony (pages 68 and 69) had just run new pace tops. However, John Paul Too was coming off a **double top** (a new pace top accompanied by at least a two point final top). Double tops normally knock a horse out for a while, and they often bounce more off a double top than just a final top of two points or more. By running its lifetime bests both early and late, the animal usually needs some time to recover.[2] Pure Harmony, on the other hand, had already hit a 75 final number back in November and had followed up with a 73+ while running his (84) pace top. He rated to bounce off the 75, and he did. But in doing so, he exhibited continuing good development by staying above his previous final tops of 71 and 71+. He looked primed for another top effort, while John Paul Too looked vulnerable. John Paul Too, a resident of the powerful John Kimmel barn, was made the 2/1 favorite. Maybe it was the outside post going two turns on the Aqueduct inner dirt that dissuaded others from betting on Pure Harmony; but, he was completely overlooked by the public. He romped to a front-end score at 13/1.

---

[2]Lightly raced horses that run double tops where the final number is below 65 are not as suspect.

EQUIFORM™ Pg: 81   **ORDAINED**   **(119)**   THE XTRAS™

9TH AQU DECEMBER 29 - 6 FURLONGS INNER DIRT

	2		3		4	
D			AQ 70"	(82)85	-->	
e	AQ 66-	(78)75	AQ 73"	(81)80	AQ ^74+	(85)81
c						
N						
o						
v	**AQ 62"** 63 **(61)**		AQ 76-	(79)78		
O					AQ 68	(75)79
c					BE 65"	(78)78
t	BE /67+w	(83)94				
S			**BE =63**	**(67)=**	BE 73+	(78)75
e	BE 66- 66	(76)76				
p			BE 73-w	(81)84		
A	SR 66+ 67	(74)76			SR 73-	(76)77
u			SR \73+	(78)70	SR /70 70	(74)77
g						
J						
u			BE 72	(79)75		
l						
J			BE 72" 73	(77)72		
u					BE 70+	(74)81
n			MP =69"	(72)=		
M						
a					BE 71+ 69	(81)87
y						
A						
p						
r						
M			AQ 72	(78)78		
a			AQ 66" 62	(61)54		
r						
F			AQ 70-w	(80)81		
e						
b			**AQ 55** 67 **(79)**			
J						
a			AQ \63	(76)75		
n						

BALTO STAR   (120)

6TH AQU JANUARY   1 - 1 MILE 7C

	2	
D		
e		
c		
N	AQ \63- 68	(82)
o		
V	AQ 64	(79) 91
O		
c		
t		
S		
e	BE 55-	(72) 77
P		

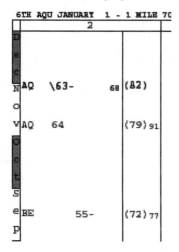

DARLING DEPUTY   (121]

2ND GPI JANUARY 14 - 7 FURLONG

	2	
D		
e		
c		
N		
o	CD 67+ 67	(79) 84
V		
O	KE -64-	(63) -
c	KE 71	(75) 79
t		
S		
e		
P		
A	SR 66	(73) 70

FIGHTING SPIRIT   (118)

6TH GPI JANUARY   5 - 7 FURLON(

	2	
D		
e		
c		
N	CR 64"	(75) 78
o		
V	CR -66+	(67) -
O		
c	CR 68- 68	(73) 69
t		
S	CR -64	(67) -
e		
P		
A	CR 65+w	(68) 75
u		
g	CR 62	(71) 78
J	CR 60"	(68) 73
u		
l		
1	CR 61+	(67) 70

MR LION HEART   (119)

FURLONGS DIRT

	3	
D	-->	
e		
c	HO 51- 50	(71) 77
N		
o		
V	SA 59"	(68) 72
O		
c		
t		

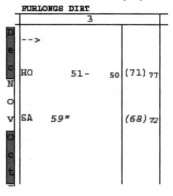

EQUIFORM™ Pg: 20 **CHASE A STAR** (114)

3RD FGX FEBRUARY 25 STATE-BRED - 1 MILE DIRT

	2		3	
D	FG 60-	(67) 68		
e				
c	LD 60"	(66) 69		
t				
S	LD 57	(60) 56		
e			-->	
F			FG 60"	(74) 80
e				
b				
J				
a			FG 61+	(68) 67

EQUIFORM™ Pg: 68 **MILLENNIUM WIND** (123)

9TH KEE APRIL 14 - 1 1/8 MILES DIRT

	2		3	
D				
e	HO 74"	69 (73)		
c				
p			-->	
r				
M				
a			FG 73	74 (82)
r				
F				
e				
b				
J			SA 74+w	68 (69)
a				

EQUIFORM™ Pg: 37   **ICICLE ANGEL   (117)**   THE XTRAS™

6TH SAX MARCH 30 - 6 1/2 FURLONGS DIRT

	2		3		4	
D e c			HO	64+	63 (67) 59		
N o v			HO	64"	63 (67) 57		
O c t							
S e p	EM	62"w	(62) 63				
A u g	EM	58+	(66) 71	EM	66+w	67 (67) 57	
g	EM	55-w	(61) 74	EM	60	62 (73) 74	
J u l				**EM**	**67**	**65 (69)**	
				EM	64	63 (64) 58	
J u n							
M a y							
A p r							
M a r						-->	
						SA	66"	66 (76)
F e b						SA	66"	66 (72)
b						SA	^63+	64 (70)

EQUIFORM™ Pg: 73   **OUTOFTHEBOX** (112)

10TH GPX FEBRUARY 17 - 1 1/16 MILES DIRT

	2		3
D			
e			
c	CR	/68-	63 (66)
N			
o			
v	CD	68	71 (83)
O			
c			
t	CR	74*	72 (76)
S			
e			
p	TP	76w	72 (79)
A			
u	EP	\72w	67 (72)
g			-->
J			
a			
n		GP 74*w	()

EQUIFORM™ Pg: 74   **BUCKLE DOWN BEN** (11'

10TH GPX FEBRUARY 17 - 1 1/16 MILES DIRT

	2		3
D			
e			
c			
N	AQ	72*	65 (72)
o			
v	LR	73w	72 (69)
O			
c	DE	66+	66 (69)
t			
S			
e	DE	/70-w	65 (67)
F			
e			-->
b			
J			
a		GP ^73-	71 (75)

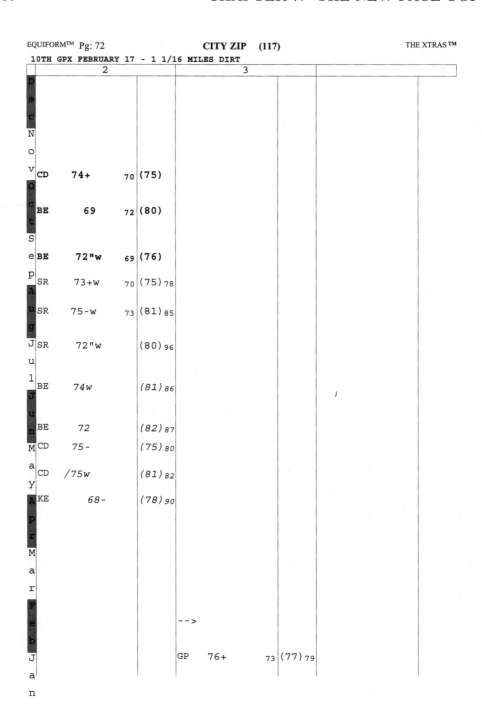

EQUIFORM™ Pg: 72   **CITY ZIP   (117)**   THE XTRAS™

10TH GPX FEBRUARY 17 - 1 1/16 MILES DIRT

	2		3		
D					
e					
c					
N					
o					
v	CD 74+	70 (75)			
O					
c	BE 69	72 (80)			
t					
S					
e	BE 72"w	69 (76)			
p	SR 73+w	70 (75) 78			
A					
u	SR 75-w	73 (81) 85			
g					
J	SR 72"w	(80) 96			
u					
l	BE 74w	(81) 86		)	
J					
u	BE 72	(82) 87			
n	CD 75-	(75) 80			
M					
a	CD /75w	(81) 82			
y	KE 68-	(78) 90			
A					
p					
x					
M					
a					
r					
F			-->		
e					
b					
J			GP 76+	73 (77) 79	
a					
n					

GLOBAL GAIT   (117)

10TH GPX FEBRUARY 17 - 1 1/16

	2		
D LR	75"w	70	(72)
e c N LR	/73-w	73	(86) 82
o v O c LR	72-w		(79) 86
t S DE	>62+		(70) 72

MEETYOUATHEBRIG   (119)

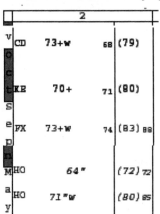

	2		
v CD	73+w	68	(79)
O c t KE	70+	71	(80)
S e FX	73+w	74	(83) 88
p n M HO	64"		(72) 72
a y HO	71"w		(80) 85

HOLIDAY THUNDER   (112)

10TH GPX FEBRUARY 17 - 1 1/16 B

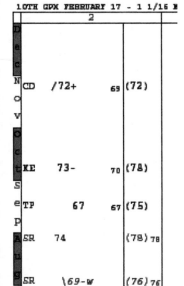

	2		
D e c N CD	/72+	69	(72)
o v O c t KE	73-	70	(78)
S e TP	67	67	(75)
P A SR	74		(78) 78
u g SR	\69-w		(76) 76

SONGANDAPRAYER   (117)

10TH GPX FEBRUARY 17 - 1 1/16 MILES DIRT

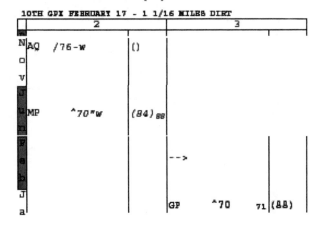

	2		3		
N AQ	/76-w	()			
o v J u MP	^70"w	(84) 88			
n F e b			-->		
J a			GP	^70	71 (88)

EQUIFORM™ Pg: 53   **JOHN PAUL TOO** **(121)**   THE XTRAS™

7TH AQU JANUARY 26 - 1 1/16 MILES INNER DIRT

D e c	2		3		4
N o v			AQ ^73+w 69 (80)		
O c t			AQ 72w 69 (75)		
			BE 71- 69 (77) 79		
S e p					
			SR 71+w (76) 77		
A u g			SR 69" 68 (73) 75		
J u l					
J u n					
M a y					
A p r			AQ /69-w 65 (77) 79		
M a r			AQ 68 (77) 78		
F e b			AQ 73+ (76) 77		
J a n			AQ 68 (76) 75 -->		
n				AQ 75+ 77 (82)	

EQUIFORM™ Pg: 55   **PURE HARMONY**   **(123)**   THE XTRAS™

7TH AQU JANUARY 26 - 1 1/16 MILES INNER DIRT

	2	3	4
D			
e			
c			
N		AQ /75w $_{73}$ (77)	
o			
v			
O		AQ 68w $_{65}$ (68)	
c			
t		BE 71+w $_{70}$ (77) $_{79}$	
S			
e			
p			
A			
u		SR 64+ (73) $_{79}$	
g			
J			
u			
l		BE 71 (81) $_{85}$	
J		BE 62+ (76) $_{82}$	
u			
n			
M			
a			
y			
A			
p			
r			
M			
a			
r			
F			
e			
b			
J		-->	
a			
n		AQ 73+ $_{78}$ (84)	

Cyclical

The new pace top is quite common with young and lightly raced horses. After all, they should run faster as they develop and mature. Older horses (four-year-olds and up), with plenty of racing experience, are another matter. Although they are still capable of running new pace tops, and often do, many have already reached their full potential or have limited upside.

One key to spotting an upcoming improvement with these more heavily raced older animals is the **cyclical pace top** (CPT).

Many older claiming horses, especially the cheaper ones, cycle in and out of form frequently. They are the racing secretary's best friend, usually available to assist him in filling races that require more betting interests. These horses are often "raced into shape", and the cyclical pace top can help us determine when a big effort is likely.

After a five-week layoff (a long one for him), Too Much Heart (page 72) was making his third start within three weeks. He had won his last three races but was now facing stronger opponents. His pace numbers had improved in his last four races, culminating with a cyclical pace top of (76) on December 14. This was the second best dirt pace number he had run in his entire career, and indicated he was in peak condition. He ran a 71" while returning $7.80.

On March 1, 2001, Madok (page 73) ran his best pace number in almost two years. He won his next start at 8/1.

The cyclical pace top occurs quite frequently, and although not as powerful as the new pace top, we have found it to be very effective when a horse makes its third start off a layoff.

As I perused the September 17, 1999 edition of the *Racing Form*, an article by Dick Jerardi aroused my interest. Jerardi's article focused on the second race at the Meadowlands on September 11, 1999. After analyzing the race, he concluded that Frank T. (page 74) was worth a wager at 3/1, citing his three out of four record at the Big M along with his affinity for the one mile and 70 yards distance. He saw no reason why the horse shouldn't fire and was aghast when Prince Tierra (page 75) won the race at almost 40/1.

I hadn't played the Meadowlands that evening. But, out of curiosity, I decided to look at The Xtras for the race. As The Xtras were printing, I noticed that two races back, Prince Tierra had broken from the twelve post going a mile at Monmouth. Then, in his next start, another route at Monmouth, he had chased a sizzling 21-4/5, 45-4/5 pace before fading badly.

When I looked at The Xtras, I was as dumbfounded as Jerardi, but from a totally different perspective. I couldn't believe that a horse coming off a cyclical pace top (74) who had run his two best fast track races (68 and 68+) at the Meadowlands paid $80.80. Two of Prince Tierra's good Meadowlands races did not appear in the *Form's* PP's due to the ten-race cutoff. While he lauded the Meadowlands record of Frank T., Jerardi downgraded Prince Tierra due to his 0/13 record over the same oval. He made the same mistake others commit by measuring wins and losses rather than performance. Prince Tierra had given every indication that he liked the Meadowlands, but this had escaped Jerardi's faulty analysis. Certainly, Frank T. had run big back numbers at the Meadowlands, but his recent form gave no indication that he was ready to run back to those numbers, an assessment which Jerardi duly acknowledged. Meanwhile, Prince Tierra had given a wake-up call with the cyclical pace top and, given his preference for the Big M, was playable at 10/1 or better.

Jerardi is a keen and insightful analyst, and I have enjoyed his articles over the years. But in this case, his information set did not yield the proper clues. The Xtras did.

EQUIFORM™ Pg: 53   **TOO MUCH HEART**   **(120)**   THE XTRAS™
8TH CRC DECEMBER 24 - 1 1/16 MILES DIRT

	3	4		5	
D e c		CR =67+	(72)=	-->	
		CR 66" 65	(69)	CR 68-w 70	(76)
N		CR =70"	(68)=	CR 68+w 68	(74)
o		CR 67+w 66	(73)74		
v		CR ^59+	(68)74		
		CR 59- 62	(64)		
O c t				CR 68-w 66	(70)
		CR =60"	(56)=	CR 66" 64	(69)
S e p		CR =65"	(67)=	CR 67 61	(64)
		CR /66- 67	(73)		
A u g		CR =69-	(63)=	CR 66" 66	(70)
		CR =69+	(70)=		
J u l		CR 64+ 64	(72)	CR 68 65	(71)
		CR =69"	(78)=		
		CR =69-	(60)=	CR 65 66	(72)
		CR 62 63	(62)		
		CR 69 64	(68)		
M a y		CR 66 63	(67)	CR 65" 68	(77)79
				GP 70 62	(63)
		HI =66+	()=	GP 69"w 66	(69)
		HI =69	()=	GP 69- 66	(69)
M a r		HI =68-	()=		
		HI 64"w 58	(64)	GP 67w 65	(72)
		HI 44+53	(67)71		
				GP 62+ 63	(74)75
				GP 64 65	(74)76
				GP 67 65	(71)74
J a n				GP =68"	(59)

EQUIFORM™ Pg: 60   **MADOK** (116)   THE XTRAS™

7TH AQU MARCH 25 - 6 FURLONGS DIRT

	5		6		7	
N			AQ ^73+w (77)75			
o	TP 73" 72 (77)74					
v						
O	CD 67 68 (71)					
c			BE 76- 74 (79)75			
t	BE 71+ 71 (77)		BE 73"w 73 (80)77			
S	BE 73+ 73 (80)74					
e	SR 72 69 (73)71		SR 71" 71 (75)73			
p			SR /72+ 70 (77)77			
A	SR 73 72 (76)75					
u	BE 71- 68 (68)		DE 69- (74)74			
g			DE 72 (75)73			
J	BE 73w 71 (74)					
u			DE /70 (79)86			
l	BE 74" (79)66		DE 70 (70)67			
J	AQ 73+ 73 (83)87		DE 72 (77)72			
u						
n	AQ 69+ (77)56					
M	AQ 72" (78)73		GP 73-w 69 (73)68		-->	
a			GP 73+ (78)74		AQ 74 (82)80	
y						
A	AQ 74 (80)75		GP 71+ 71 (76)77			
p						
r	AQ 72"w (81)77		GP 71 70 (78)76		AQ 69" (75)68	

EQUIFORM™ Pg: 1   **FRANK T.**   THE XTRAS™

	3	4	5
Dec		AQ 72-w 67 (67)	
Nov		ME 69+w 68 (74)	
	CR 67" 62 (68)	ME 72-w 65 (69)	
Oct	CR 71- 68 (71)		
		ME 71w 72 (78)	
Sep	CR 74 71 (75)	BE 61" 62 (70)	
	CR 72+w 68 (72)	ME 69- 66 (70)	--> ME 67 60 (61)
Aug	M		
	CR /70w 69 (73) 66	MP 65+ 59 (61)	MP 64w 61 (58)
	CR /70 67 (71) 71		MP 66" 62 (61)
Jul	CR /65 63 (68) 63	MP 71+ 68 (68)	
			MP 68- 65 (66)
			MP \69 65 (63)
Jun		MP /70- 66 (68)	MP 62" 63 (63)
		MP 72- 67 (69)	
May			
Apr		HI =67" ( ) =	AQ 64+ 64 (68) 64
			AQ xx ( )
Mar			AQ 66" 65 (71)
	HI 69+w 68 (69) 70	HI 71+ 65 (73)	
			AQ 69 66 (71)
	GP 66- 65 (70)		AQ \66" 62 (63)
Feb		GP =70+ (48) =	AQ 68" 70 (71)
	GP 69- 63 (70)	GP 72+ 67 (66)	AQ 69- 70 (73)
		GP 73+w 69 (71)	
Jan		GPo 72+ 64 (65)	
	GP /65- 61 (68) 68	GP ^70+ 64 (66)	AQ 70+ 70 (72)

EQUIFORM™ Pg: 2 **PRINCE TIERRA** THE XTRAS™

	3	4	5
Dec	ME 66- 65(74)	ME 62" (69)74	
Nov	ME 65+ 62(66)	ME 66 (67)54	
Oct	ME 63" 65(73)	ME 63+ 60(61)	
	ME 67- 64(67)	ME 68 61(65)	
	ME ^63" 58(65)		
	ME =61+ (68)=	ME 68+ (62)57	
Sep	ME 66- 63(67)	ME 67 65(71)	
		ME =62" (70)=	-->
		MP /74-w 71(73)	ME 68-w 65(72)
Aug			MP 61+ 62(74)
			MP 62- 61(65)
		MP =67+ (65)=	
Jul	M		
		MP 67" 64(63)	
	MP 58" 62(69)	MP 64+ (76)67	
Jun			MP 64+ 66(71)
		MP /64+ 57(57)	
May			GS 64- 62(68)
Apr		GS 66+ 65(68)	GS 64" 62(64)
		GS 65 65(65)	
		GS 65+w 63(69)	
Mar		GS 64" 61(62)	GS ^65" 63(71)
		GS 63" 64(67)	
Feb		GS 62" 61(61)	
Jan		GS 60- 64(75)	

Delayed

Sometimes, a horse will run a new pace top but not demonstrate its good condition until the second race after the pace top due to one of the following factors:

- intervening turf race

- equipment change

- excuse

- against the bias

The **delayed pace top** (DPT) is operative in these situations. One of the most powerful delay patterns is a new dirt pace top followed immediately by a turf race. The intervening turf race serves as an excellent prep, building on the animal's current good form. After demonstrating the best early foot of its career, the horse's finishing ability is enhanced with a stamina building grass effort. The third race in the pattern (back on the dirt) is the payoff, when the horse puts the conditioning benefits from both earlier races together. Of course, if the intervening turf race results in a big final number top, all bets are off. But usually, this move is employed to build both the endurance of the horse and the mutuel price for those wagering on it.

After winning off the August new pace top (67), Sandy Lass (page 77) made another new pace top (71) in November. In her next start in early December, she was thrown to the wolves, moving up to the allowance ranks to face 1/5 Voodoo Dancer. Surely, trainer and former riding star Jacinto Vasquez had no illusions about winning that particular grass race at 7-1/2 furlongs. After chasing the pace for half a mile, Sandy Lass finished next to last. However, the conditioning she received in that race, coupled with the new pace top, made her a lively possibility on the second day of the 2001 Gulfstream Park meet. Dropped back in with claimers and going seven furlongs, Sandy Lass exploded to a 65, paying $47.20.

Be on the lookout for the other delay patterns mentioned above. Although requiring some detective work, they will point out many live horses hidden from the public.

EQUIFORM™ Pg: 28   **SANDY LASS (117)**   THE XTRAS™

3RD GPX JANUARY 25 - 6 FURLONGS DIRT

	2		3			
D e c						
N o v	CR =61+	(74)=				
	CR 60"	(71)70				
O c t	CR 61"w	(67)67				
S e p						
A u g	CR 56"w	(65)76				
	CR 55"	(67)81				
J u l						
J u n	CR 56+	(64)75				
M a y	CR 51+	(61)71				
A p r						
M a r						
F e b						
J a n			-->			

GP 65w   64 (70)72

Off a Layoff

Horses that run a new pace top off a layoff of 60 days or more often provide excellent betting opportunities, especially if a weak final number accompanies the new pace top. In the sixth race at the Fairgrounds on March 5, 2001, No Its Not, who had run final numbers between 68" and 70+ in his last three races, was installed as the 8/5 favorite. Ex Who, who had run a 68 final along with a NPT in his last start, was the 4/1 second choice. However, Ex Who had been away for over a month. The conditioning benefits of the NPT tend to diminish the longer a horse is absent. After all, if the animal is in good form, the trainer should want to cash in as soon as possible. With claimers, we like to see the horse back within three weeks, but allow longer rest periods for classier animals.

Now look at Land Of Dixie (page 80). After winning two of five races (all well spaced out) as a 2yo, Land of Dixie returned from a 77-day vacation with an (82) new pace top on February 23. Trainer Tom Amoss must have liked what he saw. He entered him right back ten days later, by far the shortest rest period of his career. With a June 67 as a 2yo, and a shrewd trainer like Amoss calling the shots, we felt Land Of Dixie had a good chance to run a final number in the 68-70 range. He did just that, running a 69" for a $22.20 mutuel.

Off Tracks

Sometimes, a horse that is coming off a new pace top will run its next race on an off track. If the horse has not handled wet surfaces well in the past and runs another clinker, consider it in the second race after the NPT. Conversely, if an animal has shown a liking for off tracks and is now running over such a surface off a new pace top, give it a long look.

The third race at Santa Anita on March 1, 2001, demonstrates this principle. Having progressed nicely in her 2yo campaign, Real Paranoide (page 81) peaked with a 66 final in the mud at Golden Gate. After clipping heels and losing her rider in her 3yo debut, she ran a new pace top (75) on January 26, 2001 over a sloppy surface. Real Paranoide had earned both her best pace number and best final number on off surfaces. Coming off a new pace top and running over a muddy track on March 1, she was a steal at 15/1.

Stone Gold (page 82) is another example of a horse coming off a pace move and returning to a wet track he relishes. Note that entering this May 25, 2001 race at Belmont Park, his two best final numbers were earned on off tracks. Some players would bet him on that angle alone, but the (75) cyclical pace top in his last start was further evidence that he was in shape to deliver another good effort. He did, winning with a 72-.

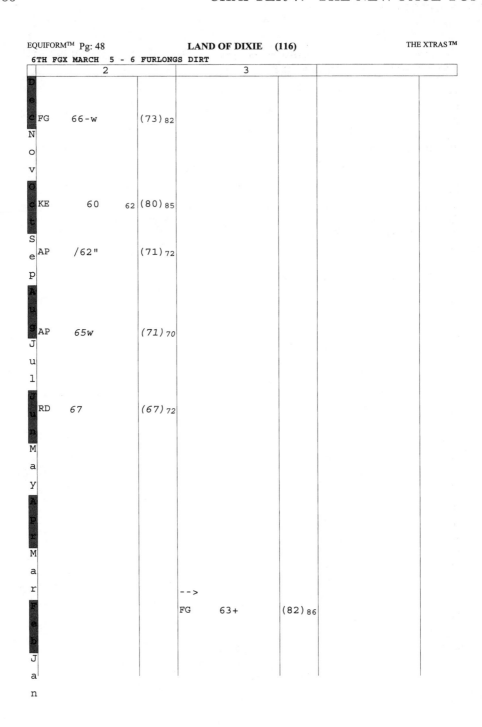

EQUIFORM™ Pg: 48   **LAND OF DIXIE   (116)**   THE XTRAS™

6TH FGX MARCH   5 - 6 FURLONGS DIRT

	2		3			

D
e
c FG   66-w   (73) 82
N
o
v
O
c KE   60   62 (80) 85
t
S
e AP   /62"   (71) 72
p
A
u
g AP   65w   (71) 70
J
u
l
J
u RD   67   (67) 72
n
M
a
y
A
p
r
M
a
r   -->
F   FG   63+   (82) 86
e
b
J
a
n

EQUIFORM™ Pg: 18   **REAL PARANOIDE**   **(116)**   THE XTRAS™

3RD SAX MARCH 1 - 6 FURLONGS DIRT

		2		3			
D							
e							
c							
N	GG	\66		(73) 72			
o							
v	**BM**	**60"**	60	**(64)**			
O							
c	BM	64"w		(69) 69			
t	BM	63"		(73) 75			
S							
e	BM	61+		(72) 71			
p	BM	60+		(67) 78			
A	SC	58		(70) 73			
u							
g	BF	58"		(63) 58			
J							
u							
l							
J							
u							
n							
M							
a							
Y							
A							
p							
r							
M							
a							
r							
F			-->				
e							
b							
J			SA /61	(75) 72			
a			SA xx	( ) 70			
n							

EQUIFORM™ Pg: 14   **STONE GOLD**   **(116)**   THE XTRAS ™

4TH BEL MAY 25 - 1 1/16 MILES DIRT

	2	3	4
Dec		AQ 69- (75) 74	
Nov			
Oct		BE 69+ 64 (70)	
Sep			
Aug			
Jul			
Jun			
May			-->
			BE 67 69 (75)
Apr			AQ 70-w 66 (68)
			AQ 69+ 64 (64)
Mar			AQ 70 69 (72)
			AQ \72 66 (71)
Feb			AQ 69" 68 (73)
			AQ 66+ 68 (66)
Jan			AQ /72+w 74 (77)
			AQ 68+ (74) 71

Out of the Blue

Although young horses often run improved pace numbers in erratic leaps, this is not the norm for older animals with plenty of racing under their girths. The **out of the blue pace top** occurs when an older, experienced horse runs a pace number at least 6 points higher than any of its last 10 pace numbers. This pattern often signals that a dramatic turnaround is imminent. It could be a back-class horse recovering from minor ailments, a trainer change, new shoes, or other factors at play. But, whatever the reason, the out of the blue pace top can help the handicapper spot these veterans that are on the upswing.

Layoff Inducing and Negative Reads

Although the new pace top is usually a positive indicator, the effort required to run so quickly in the early part of the race is sometimes detrimental. If a horse is unable to make a forward move off a lifetime pace top, something is probably amiss. We downgrade the expected performance of such animals in their second race after the new pace top unless they are coming off a double top or any of the aforementioned delay lines.

As a corollary, the new pace top can send a horse to the sidelines if it is not fit enough to withstand the stress concomitant with the NPT. If the horse is not sound, the increase in early output may cause an injury or old infirmities to resurface.

Chapter 8

Distance Switches

Horses stretching out or turning back in distance are often difficult to evaluate using standard handicapping information. Will a sprinter be able to ration his speed going two turns? How will a router fare at 6-1/2 furlongs?

THE XTRAS provide the data that will enable the user to make more informed decisions regarding distance switches.

Many handicappers erroneously reason that closing sprinters are good bets to stretch out, assuming the added ground will give them more time to display their closing kick. This is usually not the case. Unless the sprinter has displayed a degree of tactical speed, he will usually not be able to establish a prominent enough early position at the longer distance, and will be out-finished by the experienced routers.

On the other hand, sprinters with good tactical speed often make solid plays on the stretch-out. If able to ration their energy early, while getting on or near the lead, these types can often have enough left in the stretch to get the job done.

When evaluating horses stretching out for the first time, several factors should be considered. Pedigree, tactical speed, the trainer's success rate with the move, and the likely pace scenario should all be analyzed. But, as usual, the most important factor is the horse's current **condition**.

If a horse is coming off a new pace top in a sprint, has a competitive pace number, and an acceptable distance pedigree, he will probably handle his first route assignment quite nicely, often at generous odds.

Another pattern to look for with these stretch-out horses revolves around their pace/final number spreads. The **dirt spread** is simply the difference between the pace and final number (pace number minus final number), and can be positive or negative.

Take a look at Northend (page 87) as he appeared on February 16, 2001, in the 8th race at Gulfstream Park, a NW2 allowance race at a mile and a sixteenth. In his maiden voyage at Calder, he ran a spread of plus 8-1/2 (72 - 63-1/2). In his next three sprints, his spreads were +8, +6, and +1 (it is fine to round off these spreads). Do you see a pattern?

In each subsequent sprint, the spread between his pace and final numbers decreased. The progression is not always this orderly, but one wants to see the more recent sprint spreads lower than the earlier ones. Northend, trained by Larry Pilotti (who excels at the sprint to route maneuver), was improving his final numbers while learning to distribute his energy later in the race, and had an excellent chance to turn in a strong performance. Look for these **tightening spreads** in dirt stretch-out situations. Although Northend ran a new final top while defeating the 4/5 favorite Mongoose, he wound up second to You Know Who.

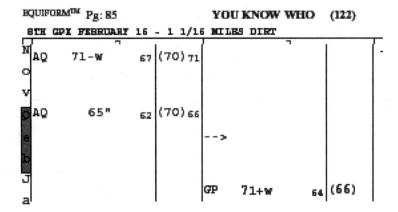

EQUIFORM™ Pg: 81   **NORTHEND** **(118)**

8TH GPI FEBRUARY 16 - 1 1/16 MILES DIRT

	2		3	
D CR	71"w	(77) 77		
e c CR	66"	(74) 77		
g J CR	/63"w	(72) 80		
e			-->	
b J a			GP ^72-	71 (73) 73

EQUIFORM™ Pg: 85   **YOU KNOW WHO** **(122)**

8TH GPI FEBRUARY 16 - 1 1/16 MILES DIRT

N O V AQ	71-w	67 (70) 71		
c AQ	65"	62 (70) 66		
e			-->	
b J a			GP 71+w	64 (66)

Reversals

You Know Who (page 87), the winner of the above Gulfstream allowance race, exhibited another stretch-out pattern, the **reversal**. The reversal is a powerful subset of the tightening spread. Most dirt horses, especially sprinters, tend to run faster pace numbers than final numbers. The reversal defines a horse that, for the first time in its career, runs a better dirt final number than pace number. In his first two races, both sprints, You Know Who ran a (+5) in his debut followed by a (-1). The reversal in his second race set him up nicely for his first route attempt, where he ran a (-5), while running a final number $\frac{1}{2}$ point better than his 2yo top. This is a great pattern for a young router, and although outrun early, You Know Who kicked in late to beat Northend by three widening lengths, earning a 74+ with Mongoose a distant third.

Later in the Gulfstream meet, the reversal pointed out a low-priced overlay. In the seventh race on March 14, the three top choices in a 1-1/16 mile allowance race were This Fleet Is Due (6/5), Distilled (5/2) and Thunder Blitz (4/1) (see pages 90–91) .

This Fleet Is Due was coming off a big double top, and figured to back up a bit. Thunder Blitz had a nice look, but had little tactical speed, and had yet to run faster than 73+. Distilled, meanwhile, had run an (83) pace top in his first start as a 3yo. As expected, he improved his final number in his next race, while tightening his dirt spread to (+1). He followed that up with a reversal (-3), and was clearly the horse to beat. He assumed command at the start and romped home by almost five lengths.

The reversal is also potent for horses with limited route experience. All the horses on pages 92−94 turned in winning efforts off the reversal. Note the new pace top on Driven Force preceding the reversal. This is a dynamite look for a stretch-out horse, combining two strong patterns back-to-back. Berchtesgaden, exhibits a **delayed reversal** due to the intervening turf race. Giving Noreen is similar to You Know Who, reversing early in her 3yo season while running right in line with her 2yo final top.

Look at Powerful Package in the eighth race at Aqueduct on April 19, 2001. After breaking through his four-year-old final top with a

68/73- reversal on March 16 at Gulfstream, Powerful Package was sent to Hialeah for a grass race, finishing last in a field of seven.[1] Shipped back north to Aqueduct for his next start, his good dirt form was partially concealed. Coming off the delayed reversal, he rallied strongly to win by two lengths, running a 74 and returning $29.40.

---

[1]In this textual format (68/73-), the pace number comes before the slash (/) and the final number after.

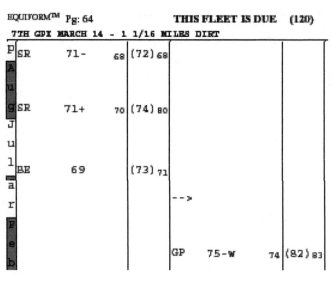

EQUIFORM™ Pg: 64   **THIS FLEET IS DUE**   **(120)**

7TH GDI MARCH 14 - 1 1/16 MILES DIRT

SR	71-	68 (72) 68	
SR	71+	70 (74) 80	
BE	69	(73) 71	
		-->	
		GP 75-w	74 (82) 83

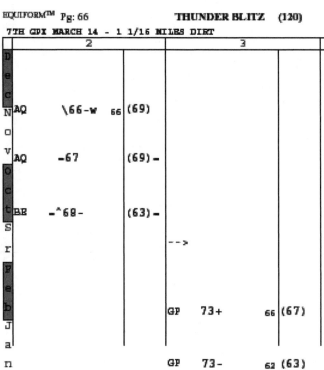

EQUIFORM™ Pg: 66   **THUNDER BLITZ**   **(120)**

7TH GDI MARCH 14 - 1 1/16 MILES DIRT

2		3	
AQ \66-w 66 (69)			
AQ -67 (69) -			
BE -^68- (63) -			
-->			
		GP 73+ 66 (67)	
		GP 73- 62 (63)	

EQUIFORM™ Pg: 67	**DISTILLED (120)**	THE XTRAS™

7TH GPX MARCH 14 - 1 1/16 MILES DIRT

	2		3			
D e c	AQ 70"	(78)$_{80}$				
N o	AQ 73w	(78)$_{84}$				
V **O** c **t**	**AQ =66"**	**(70)=**				
S e **P**	**BE** 69	$_{68}$**(72)**				
A u **g**	SR *55"*	*(61)*$_{73}$				
J u l						
J **u** **n**						
M a y						
A **P** **r**						
M a r		-->				
F **e** **b**		**GP 75-**	$_{68}$**(72)**			
J a		**GP 75+**	$_{68}$**(76)**			
n		GP 73"	$_{72}$ (83)$_{88}$			

EQUIFORM™ Pg: 14   **DRIVEN FORCE**   **(121)**   THE XTRAS™

3RD SAX FEBRUARY 7 - 1 MILE DIRT

Month	3	4	5
D		SA 71" 72 (81)	
e			
c	HO 66" 65 (76) 76	HO 71+ 71 (79) 76	
N			
o	HO 68" (70) 70	HO 66" (68) 71	
v			
O	SA 67 66 (72) 67	SA =68" (67) =	
c			
t	SA 69-w 67 (76) 72		
S	SA 63+ (75) 75	SA 66- 66 (70) 70	
e	FX 65" 64 (75) 77	FX 70 70 (75) 80	
p			
A			
u	DM *66* (69) 67	DM 69" (78) 77	
g			
J	DM 60- 60 (72) 72	DM 70" (73) 66	
u			
l		HO 68+ (72) 69	
J	HO 65 65 (71) 66	**HO =67** (63) =	
u			
n			
M		**HO =66+** (58) =	
a			
y			
A		SA =69+ (72) =	
p	SA 60+ 60 (68) 68	SA =66 (75) =	
r			
M			
a	**SA 62- 63 (69)**	SA =69- (74) =	
r	SA 64 (73) 67		
F		**SA =^69** (61) =	
e			
b	SA 66- (70) 69		-->
J			
a	SA 63+ 63 (71) 65		
n	SA 59" 61 (72) 68		**SA 73** 65 (65)

EQUIFORM™ Pg: 46   **BERCHTESGADEN   (118)**

7TH AQU APRIL   1 - 1 1/8 MILES DIRT

	2		3	
D				
e				
c	AQ 65-	(73) 74		
N	AQ 64 "	63 (69) 69		
o				
v				
O				
c				
t	BE ^65-	62 (66)		
S	BE 61	(67) 53		
M			-->	
a				
r				
F				
e				
b			PG -6 9+	(63) -
J				
a				
n			AQ 63"w 54 (54)	

EQUIFORM™ Pg: 60   **GIVING NOREEN   (121)**

8TH AQU FEBRUARY 14 - 1 1/16 MILES INNER DIRT

	2		3	
D	AQ 66+	62 (69)		
e	AQ /69"	(82) 87		
c				
N				
o				
v	AQ 68 "	(74) 83		
e			-->	
b				
J				
a			AQ 69"w 64 (68)	

EQUIFORM™ Pg: 62   **POWERFUL PACKAGE   (122)**   THE XTRAS™

8TH AQU APRIL 19 - 1 MILE DIRT

	3	4	5
D e c		AQ 68 (76)$_{75}$ **AQ 62- $_{63}$(71)**	
N o v			
O c t		AQ 67" (74)$_{76}$ BE 70- $_{69}$(72)$_{69}$	
S e p			
p		BE 72- (76)$_{77}$	
A u g			
J u l			
J u n			
M a y			
A p r		AQ /66+ $_{64}$(71)	-->
M a r			**HI =^68" ()=**
		AQ 66+ (77)$_{79}$	**GP 73-w $_{66}$(68)**
F e b		AQ 65-w (71)$_{70}$	
		AQ 66 (74)$_{73}$	**GP =70" (66)=**
J a n	**AQ 68- $_{65}$(70)**		GP ^60 $_{61}$(72)$_{76}$

The Turnback

When considering dirt horses turning back in distance, The Xtras are an invaluable tool for snaring long shot winners.

The most common turnback situations occur with horses going from a route to a sprint. However, they can also be found with horses cutting back from 6-1/2 or 7 furlongs to 6 furlongs. The **turnback number** (found to the left of the four furlong pace number) represents six-furlong variant-adjusted velocity. When horses fade, sometimes severely, in races longer than six furlongs, the final numbers do not illuminate how the horse performed until the $\frac{3}{4}$ mile mark. But The Xtras provide this information for dirt races beyond six furlongs.

On January 24, 2000, at Aqueduct, the turnback struck in consecutive races. The third race was a six-horse affair for 3yo colts going six furlongs for a $35,000 tag. Holy Cannoli was the 3/5 favorite, followed by Wrestler at 2/1, and Quick Sez Me at 4/1. Compelling Dance (page 97) dismissed at 25/1, was a vintage turnback play. Although the three top choices had all run faster final numbers than his best of 67-, Compelling Dance had earned a 69 turnback number in his November win at the Meadowlands. He bounced horribly off that big double top and was given a short vacation. Compelling Dance's turnback number was the second best 6f number in the race. After rating off the early pace, he won by two lengths, returning $52.50.

In the very next race, the best final number any of the nine contestants had run was a 67", and only Love's Arrow (page 97) had run a turnback number better than that figure. But what a turnback number it was! After setting a pressured pace on December 15, 2000 in his first route try, Love's Arrow faded to a 64 final. But the 71 turnback number he earned in that race towered over the competition he was facing at six furlongs in his 4yo debut. I must confess that I bet him in his next route attempt on December 29, even though he drew post position eleven. The (83) new pace top was staring me in the face, but I knew he might bounce off such a big **internal top** (the 71 turnback number) coming back on short rest. He did. After chasing the pace from his outside post, Love's Arrow gave way and finished a distant eighth.

Then, almost a month later, trainer Richard Schosberg placed him back in a sprint. Schosberg has been very successful with the route to sprint move over the years, and I felt confident Love's Arrow was a strong play at almost 7/1. He paid $15.80.

The sixth race at Bay Meadows on May 2, 2001 is another good illustration of the turnback number in action. Two horses stood out on The Xtras. Both Sourcebook and Miss Blue Bayou (page 98) were off new pace tops and both had run recent 66 turnback numbers. Sourcebook's 66 turnback number was only $\frac{3}{4}$ points higher than her associated final number, whereas Miss Blue Bayou's 66 turnback number was 4-1/4 points better than her respective final number. This is a recipe for value, as the public tends to focus on final numbers. As post time neared, Sourcebook was 6/5 and Miss Blue Bayou 8/1. In Northern California, it's not often one gets ace Russell Baze at 8/1 on a legitimate contender, but I did here due to the hidden turnback number. Miss Blue Bayou won by 2-1/2 lengths, paying $18.00, with Sourcebook second to complete a most generous $51.20 exacta.

EQUIFORM™ Pg: 21   **COMPELLING DANCE**   **(111*)**

3RD AQU JANUARY 24 - 6 FURLONGS INNER DIRT

	2		3	
D				
e				
c				
N				
o	AQ	50 60	(66)	
v	ME	67-w 69	(79)	
O				
c	ME	61+ 60	(72)	
t				
S	BE	58+	(69) 77	
e				
P				
A	SR	49	(63) 69	

EQUIFORM™ Pg: 30   **LOVE'S ARROW**   **(121)**

4TH AQU JANUARY 24   STATE-BRED - 6 FURLONGS INNER DIRT

	2		3	
D			AQ 59 59	(67)
e			AQ 64 71	(83)
c				
N			AQ 55	(68) 81
o				
v				
O				
c			BE 60+ 60	(69) 71
t				
S			BE 65"	(73) 79
e				

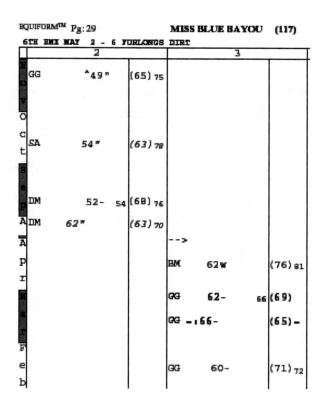

EQUIFORM™ Pg: 33   **SOURCEBOOK (117)**

6TH BMX MAY 2 - 6 FURLONGS DIRT

	2	3
y TU		
A		-->
p TU --		
r SA		
		SA 65+ 66 (82) 88
		SA \64 (74) 83
		SA *63" 65 (80) 86
		SA /58" (80) 90

EQUIFORM™ Pg: 29   **MISS BLUE BAYOU (117)**

6TH BMX MAY 2 - 6 FURLONGS DIRT

	2	3
GG *49" (65) 75		
O		
c SA 54" (63) 78		
t		
DM 52- 54 (68) 76		
A DM 62" (63) 70		
A		-->
p		BM 62w (76) 81
r		GG 62- 66 (69)
		GG -166- (65) -
F		
e		GG 60- (71) 72
b		

Chapter 9

Lightly Raced Horses

One of the more surprising discoveries of our research involves lightly raced *dirt* horses (lightly raced turf horses will be covered later). As expected, we found that pace numbers were crucial in evaluating lower level maiden claiming races, especially when the horse with the best pace number(s) was dropping from a maiden special weight event on the same circuit.

Maiden claiming races are often captured by horses with a touch of class that are able to get the lead early and, thus, discourage the perennial losers. Be hesitant to dismiss any animal that rates to secure an early uncontested lead in these events, even if its final numbers look weaker. A decent mutuel may be in the offing.

The big surprise came when we analyzed maiden special weight and preliminary allowance races. In these affairs, early pace was not nearly as important and, to our amazement, we found that standard pace analysis wasn't very enlightening. In fact, with horses that had only one or two races, using conventional pace methods could be downright misleading.

There are various reasons for this phenomenon. First of all, many trainers don't go all out with their first-time starters (or second- and third-timers for that matter). These trainers prefer to give them a race or two before cracking down.

In New York, trainer Nick Zito typifies this approach. Having won the Kentucky Derby with late developers Strike The Gold and Go For

Gin, Zito has a low strike rate with first-time starters. He elects to let most of them "stretch their legs" while getting exposure to the components of real competition (dirt kicked in their faces, running between horses, etc). Zito will have a live first-timer now and then, but it is not his forte.

Turf legends like Charlie Whittingham and Mack Miller were of the same ilk, able to get a horse to peak for a specific engagement, but rarely willing to sacrifice long-term goals for short-term laurels. By studying how different trainers handle their younger stock, the handicapper will be able to more effectively predict the performance of these newcomers.

On the major circuits, the frequent presence of several first-time starters sporting high auction prices and flashy pedigrees adds more uncertainty. If ready to roll in their debuts (check the trainer's proficiency with first-timers), these types can wreak havoc with any pace analysis. Although trainer tendencies, pedigree analysis, and healthy tote board action can provide clues, we have found some patterns that consistently provide value in these situations.

Plunge Lines

The first pattern, which is more powerful in maiden claimers, is the drop-off or **plunge line**. When a first-time starter runs a pace number that is 15 or more points better than its final number, it was either (a) giving an honest effort or (b) out for exercise and not "asked" for anything in the latter stages of the race. These "pop and stop" types can run dramatically improved final numbers next time out by rationing their energy more evenly and/or facing weaker competition.

Both Coach Tobacco and Secret Liaison (page 103) ran plunge lines in their debuts. After running 76/55 in a maiden special weight event, Coach Tobacco dropped into a maiden claimer three weeks later to post a $56.50 upset. Secret Liaison also began in a maiden special race, running an 81/63. When she returned two weeks later at the same level, her 91 two-furlong number coupled with an (81) pace number looked dominant, and she never looked back to the tune of $45.80.

The plunge line is particularly lucrative with one-number horses that are dropping from an open maiden special weight race to a maiden claimer while possessing the "boss" pace number.

Before discussing the really surprising discovery mentioned earlier, let's refer to traditional pace handicapping as a backdrop. Look at the following fractional splits of imaginary horses A and B.

Horse A	22.0	45.1	1:10.3
Horse B	22.5	45.8	1:10.3

Conventional pace theory would suggest that, all else being equal, Horse A, due to his superior early pace ability, would usually defeat Horse B. Remember, **EQUIFORM** pace numbers should be primarily used to evaluate **condition**, not pace match-ups. In any event, the standard theory does have some validity when dealing with older, experienced horses. Their general abilities and running styles are well established and, in this scenario, match-up analysis has some merit. But who would pretend that they could pick representative pace lines for a bunch of second- and third-time starters. We humbly admit that our crystal ball told us to "ask again later".

However, we did discover another pattern (or line) that is quite revealing regarding second-time starters (sometimes, even for third- or fourth-time starters). Before elucidating this pattern, we will touch upon another important concept, energy distribution. Our research shows that most horses, especially routers, run their best final numbers when they distribute their energy evenly. If a horse has run a 73 final number accompanied by an (85) pace number, he will probably run a better final number down the road when he runs a lower pace number.

This is not news. Several others have reached the same conclusion, and the research is well documented. The more energy expended early, the less available later. Or, in handicapping parlance, as pace numbers increase, the associated final numbers tend to decrease. Of course, this is not universal but, on balance, it is a sound conclusion. Horses do usually maximize final time by distributing their energy evenly throughout the race. That is why several top jockeys, notably Pat Day, exhibit such splendid timing.

Despite some questionable rides on Easy Goer, a personal favorite of ours, Day is a master of pace and energy distribution. Give us a race loaded with speed at 6-1/2 or 7 furlongs, with Day on a competitive stalker or closer, and he will rarely disappoint. Of course, neither will Bailey, Stevens, or Eddie D. But when it comes to rationing the speed of a frontrunner, Day is the master. He allows them to run naturally in the early part of the race, getting them to the top, but then, when pressured by other horses, he does not push his mount too soon. In fact, oftentimes, another horse will overtake him for the lead, but Day will come charging back on the inside to win. Day either has a PhD in energy distribution or an intuitive sense of how to get a horse to relax. He understands better than most riders that the efficient distribution of energy maximizes final time, and he possesses the uncommon skill to pull it off.

COACH TOBACCO   (120)

VGS DIRT

-->	-
AQ 55	(76) 81

SECRET LIAISON   (117)

6 FURLONGS DIRT - Three Year C

	3	
-	-->	
	HO 63	(81) 91

AFFAIRINTHEFOREST   (117)

6 FURLONGS DIRT - Three Year (

	3	
-->		
HO 70 "	70	(78) 83
SA 70+	68	(76) 78

FLYLIKETHEWIND   (117)

6 FURLONGS DIRT - Three Year (

	3	
-->		
HO 70-		(68) 57

EQUIFORM™ P₈: 36   **RON CHERRY   (117)**

7TH RACE HOL MAY 13TH   - 6 FURLONGS DIRT - Three Year (

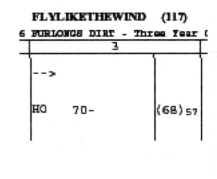

	2		3	
O	SA *67 "	67 (74) 78		
c				
t	SA 66	(72) 79		
S				
e	DM 63+	(69) 74		
-			-->	
V				
A				
p				
r				
M			SA 69+	67 (73) 65

Compression Lines

So what does all of this have to do with second time starters? Well, just as the plunge line describes first-time starters who dissipate excess energy early in the race, the **compression line** isolates horses that evenly distribute their energy in their debuts. The compression line defines horses that run dirt spreads of 4 points or less in their opening race (i.e., between -4 and +4). These compression horses are ready to explode and often "light up" the tote-board.

The beauty of these compression horses from a wagering perspective is that standard pace analysis usually leads its practitioners elsewhere. Consider the following two imaginary first-time starters, who broke their maidens going seven panels in MSW events at Belmont Park. Let's assume they ran on the same day, carried equal weight, got the same inside trip, and ran the same final time over a surface that didn't change. As can be seen by the Equiform numbers below, Horse A set a much quicker pace:

	Final	6F	4F	2F
Horse A	71	71	(80)	84
Horse B	71	70	(71)	74

If these two horses were to meet in a preliminary allowance race a few weeks later, traditional pace handicappers would favor Horse A due to his superior pace number. However, when evaluating one-number horses, this is simply not the case. Second-time-out compression horses, with a competitive final number, will usually defeat other one-number horses with a better pace figure.

The empirical evidence piqued our curiosity, and we sought a rational explanation for this counter-intuitive result. Horses that win first out have usually been geared up to deliver a top effort. With this in mind, we revisited the "bounce" theory and wondered if it might somehow apply to first-time starters. After all, if a horse often bounces after a big effort off a layoff, why couldn't it bounce off its first race? In a sense, first time out could be considered to be running off a layoff.

Then, we looked at the relative distribution of the pace and final numbers of first-time starters. Horses running compression lines in their opening race backed up much less frequently than horses that didn't. Compression horses, whether they won their first race or not, usually have more latent ability. They will often exhibit dramatic bursts of energy at some juncture in their second start, sometimes even dueling superior pace figure horses into defeat. Their energy has been bottled up or "compressed", and, when asked to release their reserves, their performances can be devastating.

The seventh race at Hollywood Park on May 13, 2001, nicely illustrates the explosive potential of compression horses. In a six-furlong event for three-year-olds and up, bred in California, Affairintheforset was installed as the 4/5 favorite, with both Flylikethewind and Ron Cherry at 4/1 (see page 103). Affairintheforest was on a decent line, improving both his pace and two furlong numbers in his second start, while improving slightly to a 70" final. Ron Cherry had shown steady progress in his four starts, and was coming off a six-week layoff after recording a 69+. Both of these horses had done nothing wrong in their brief careers, but neither one had the next out potential of Flylikethewind, who had run a 68/70- compression line in his debut. Although apparently overmatched in the pace department, Flylikethewind breezed right to the top under jockey Alex Solis and held off a late rally from the favorite to win by a head, earning an 81/74". When lightly raced compression horses get the lead, they are tough to run down.

Horses that run compression or plunge lines first time out are likely to improve in their second starts. Remember, a plunge line denotes at least a 15 point drop-off, while compression is 4 points or less. However, the pace/final number distribution of most first-timers falls somewhere in between, and they are trickier to evaluate. But even with these types, we have found a pattern that is quite useful as it allows us to wager *against* several impressive debut winners.

Negative Spreads

The **negative spread** defines a first-time starter on the dirt who runs a spread greater than plus four points, but less than plus 15 (4 < dirt spread < 15), while running an acceptable race for the class level. On the major circuits, an acceptable race is defined as a 65 or better final number (at lesser tracks, this acceptable final number is lower).

When first-timers run fast early *and* late, they normally regress second time out. Here are some representative negative spreads (with the pace number first) for these types of horses.

4F	Final
83	72
77	69
75	66
77	70

Several horses that run negative spreads first time out do return to win and/or improve their final numbers. Maybe one ran a 76/70, but was eased up in the final eighth of a mile, while winning by 10 lengths. Had this animal been kept to the task, it may have run a 76/73 and become a compression horse. We are not in the business of speculating on such matters. What we do know is that these negative spread horses, if not given a rest (preferably 30 days or more), are poor wagering propositions, especially if the spread is in the seven to ten point range. They probably gave an honest effort first time out and, the bigger the final number, the more likely to back up.

Compression horses also make good plays against faster final figure horses off tops. In the second race at Aqueduct on April 14, 2001 (see page 108), the odds-on favorite, Hollywood Bull, had run a big double top off a sixteen-month layoff and would probably bounce. Longonot (at 5/1) was also off a double top. Meanwhile, High Commissioner (5/2) had run a 72/69- compression line in his debut, was getting seven pounds from Hollywood Bull, and rated to move forward. As it turned out, I didn't make much on the race as I bet Southern Classic (at 26/1 off a new pace top) along with High Commissioner. High Commisioner won by almost five lengths while Southern Classic, after being bumped at the start, ran dead last.

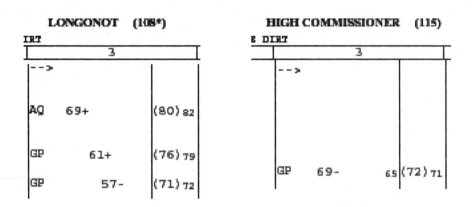

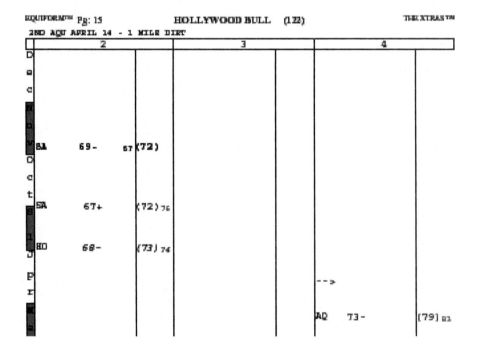

Chapter 10

Turf Racing

Did you ever see the movie "The Godfather"? Did you ever read the novel? They have much in common, but no discerning audience would ever confuse one with the other. They are two distinct art forms to be understood and appreciated in quite different ways. The same is true for dirt and turf racing. Consequently, the analysis of turf races requires a unique paradigm, which will be detailed after a brief historical perspective.

Many racing scholars consider St Simon, foaled in 1881, to be the greatest thoroughbred horse of all time. Unable to compete in the English classics due to a quirk in the racing laws (a horse was not eligible to compete if its owner had died before the race), St Simon was undefeated in ten races, often winning by twenty lengths or more while under stout restraint. His regular rider, Fred Archer, the best jockey of 19th century England, and his trainer, Matthew Duncan, were both associated with several classic horses. Archer would later ride the 16-time winner and undefeated English Triple Crown champion Ormonde, but still thought that St Simon was in a league by himself. Duncan claimed that St Simon was as good at one furlong as he was at three miles, and trained him to win at distances from six furlongs to the 2-1/2 miles of the Ascot Gold Cup.

Unlike many top class horses, St Simon went on to an outstanding career at stud. He was the leading sire nine times and the top brood-mare sire six times. In 1900, his sons and daughters captured all five of the English classics (2000 Guineas, Derby, St Leger, 1000 Guineas and the Oaks). But for some time, St Simon's direct male descendants were unable to pass on the superior traits of their ancestor, and the St Simon line was in danger of dying out until Prince Rose surfaced. Prince Rose was killed by artillery fire during the Normandy invasion, but his progeny breathed new life into the St Simon line. His best-known son, Princequillo, had been fortuitously transported to the United States a few years earlier.

Princequillo was a long distance specialist, but also passed on a fair amount of speed to his descendants. With the possible exception of Northern Dancer, Princequillo has had the greatest impact on American turf breeding over the last 50 years. From his sons Prince John and Round Table came Poker, Stage Door Johnny, King's Bishop and numerous others who have left an indelible mark on turf pedigrees. Princequillo was also a very productive broodmare sire, with the legendary Secretariat being his crowning achievement in that arena.

At **EQUIFORM**, we are not experts on pedigrees, conformation, webbed feet, the proverbial "daisy cutting action", or other genetic factors that produce good turf runners. But we do know how to apply our numbers to identify horses that will perform well on the turf.

Early speed, usually an asset on the dirt, is not nearly as beneficial on the grass. In fact, the distinguishing feature of most good grass horses is the ability to distribute the bulk of their energy late in the race. That is why our grass pace numbers tend to be lower than their dirt counterparts. Equiform doesn't normalize turf pace numbers to make them comparable with dirt pace numbers. That would mask the very essence of turf racing. By reporting the actual, variant-adjusted velocities, Equiform is able to properly evaluate the real dynamics of racing on the green.

Top grass riders usually show restraint (sometimes, too much), favoring a good trip near the inside over prominent early position. Having rationed their mount's energy, these superior riders have a knack for unleashing its reserves at just the right time. Without a doubt, riding on the lawn requires more skill than riding on the dirt. Backing apprentices or weak riders on the dirt, especially in sprints, is often not a problem. After all, if the horse is the speed of the race and in condition, all the apprentice has to do is get him cleanly out of the gate and hang on. It doesn't work that way on the grass. Superior grass riders possess patience, a keen sense of pace, and the courage to accelerate through a momentary opening. These skills take time to master. That is why bug-boys and less skilled riders win such a low percentage of grass races on the major circuits.

Turf Pace Lows and the TD Line

Given these major differences between dirt and turf racing, Equiform employs a unique methodology for each surface. While the new pace top is the most common dirt pattern signaling improved condition, its corollary on the turf is the **turf pace low**.

The new pace top isolates horses that are running better in the most stressful segment of dirt races. The turf pace low (TPL) serves a similar purpose in grass races. The "real racing" in most grass affairs usually occurs after the first half mile has already been run (short turf sprints excluded). The ability to accelerate late in the race is the key to success on the turf, and **THE XTRAS** provide data to help the handicapper assess this ability.

The **turf decline line** is a potent subset of the turf pace low. The turf decline line (TD line) is defined as a decrease in successive turf pace numbers of at least six points to a turf pace low, with the associated final numbers within two points of each other. This pattern points out horses that are noticeably improving their finishing ability. If they are going slower early, but running roughly the same final number, they are finishing better. This is a powerful conditioning angle on the weeds.

Take a look at Stetson Lady (page 116) in the fourth race at Santa Anita on March 29, 2001. She opened her five year-old campaign with three finals right around 70, and didn't improve much until December, when she hit a 73- final top. After a 74/70 to start 2001, she ran a 64/71- in her next race. The big drop to a turf pace low (64) while running almost the same final number is a particularly strong pattern. It is analogous to a significant pace top on the dirt.

Stetson Lady was sitting on a big effort. The public made Guthrun (page 117) the favorite at 2/1, followed by Glorious Linda (page 118) at 3/1. Neither of them had run a faster final number than Stetson Lady's 73-, and more importantly, did not exhibit any condition patterns. Maybe the presence of Revillew Slew and Salish Slew, also front-running types, suggested Stetson Lady would be compromised by the pace scenario. However, we have learned that horses in top form often overcome these match-up or race-shape deficiencies. Stetson Lady stalked the early leader, Salish Slew, battled that one through the stretch, and got up by a neck at $26.20. Guthrun, as is her wont, broke slowly, and was never a factor, while Glorious Linda was a late-rallying third.

The eighth race at the Fairgrounds on January 6, 2001, featured an extremely competitive field going about a mile on the grass. On strictly a final number basis, six or seven horses appeared capable of hitting 73 to 74. The crowd had such difficulty sorting them out, that Frankly Classic was established as the tepid favorite at almost 9/2. But there was only one horse, Eltawaasul (page 119) coming off a TD line. Note the drop-off to a new TPL. Nat's Big Party also had a nice look, coming off a **cyclical pace low** (CPL) of 51 (page 120). Since Eltawaasul was a lightly raced 5yo with more upside potential, I bet him to win and boxed him with Nat's Big Party in the exacta. The following comments from the January 14, 2001 *Racing Form Charts Weekly* tell the story.

> **Eltawaasul** saved ground early, moved out before the second turn, rallied five wide turning for home, and out-kicked **Private Power** to the wire. Private Power settled early, rallied five wide around the second turn, closed gamely and was out-kicked to the wire. **Nat's Big Party**, unhurried early, split foes while advancing around the second turn, angled out for the drive, closed gamely but was too late.

Note that the chart caller used the phrases "out-kicked" and "closed gamely". This finishing ability delivers the goods on the grass.

A spectacular example of the turf pace low occurred on February 16, 2001 in the fourth race at Gulfstream Park (see pages 121-122). The 9/5 public choice, Afternoon Rose, was off a final number top and rated to bounce back to the 68/69 area. I was looking for a filly that could get to that range at a better price. Certainly, coming off a turf pace low with some good 2yo final numbers to back it up, Candy Mint had to be played at 4/1. But two other horses intrigued me. Where's Cielo was on a TD line with some 67's as a 2yo, and Tanallover had just run a turf pace low with a 66- as a 2yo. It is not uncommon for young horses to move up a few final points off these patterns, so I also placed small win wagers on these two long shots. Tanallover improved to a 68" final and paid $186.40. Any method can tab a long shot now and then, but knowing that the TD line or the TPL can produce this type of explosion will enable you to envision some of these "bombs" on the grass.

As with the new pace top on the dirt, the TPL or TD line may be operative off a delay (intervening dirt race, excuse, layoff, etc). After debuting with a 65/63- on the Saratoga lawn, Fiddle (page 123) turned in two dismal runs on the dirt. Trainer Allen Jerkens returned her to the grass in a stakes race, and Fiddle responded with a 54/64", creating a TD line. After a freshening, Fiddle resurfaced in a maiden special race at Gulfstream Park on January 7, 2001, and paid $48.00 while advancing to a 69+ final. Horses can improve dramatically between their two and three year-old seasons, and the TD line provides a big clue as to the timing of these moves.

Whenever a horse runs a turf pace low, one should give it a second look. Neither Castle Comer (page 124) nor Answer To Me (page 125), was on a TD line in the following examples (the final number difference of successive grass races was not two points or less), but both were off **delayed pace lows**.

After a running a TPL (55) on June 18, Castle Comer followed up with a dirt pace top on June 27 while fading badly. Returned to the weeds, he won comfortably at 3/1 while improving to a 70+.

Answer To Me was coming off a double delay after a mid-August TPL (50). Note that he reversed in his September dirt race (a good sign for a grass horse), and after another dirt effort, was put back on the grass on November 2, and won by almost five lengths.

Horses making their first start on grass require special handling. Ten or twenty years ago, a handicapper with access to good pedigree information enjoyed a sizable edge in these situations. Whether it was

Tomlinson ratings (now available in the *Racing Form*), Bloodstock Research's American Produce Records (then a 20 volume set – now available on CD ROM) or consulting trainer statistics, a player willing to do the work could find some superb plays. Obviously, as this information became more available to the public, its wagering value diminished.

These guides are still helpful, but there are other ways to retain an edge with first time grass horses. Identifying superior grass sires before they become well known via Tomlinson etc can be a rewarding first step. If you take the time to peruse the result charts of grass races around the country, you will sometimes notice a relatively obscure sire producing a few turf winners at boxcar mutuels. Be on the lookout for the progeny of these sires before they are tabulated in the guides and made available to the public. This approach with Diesis and several others allowed me to cash several nice tickets before their ability for producing good grass runners became well established.

The second and more common method is to use the Equiform numbers to predict which horses are likely to handle the surface switch effectively. Since success on the grass usually requires the late distribution of energy, we prefer horses that have exhibited that tendency on the dirt, as long as they have some semblance of a grass pedigree.

Lightly raced horses that run compression lines on the dirt are often able to adapt immediately to the demands of turf racing. So too are older horses that frequently run dirt pace numbers lower than their final numbers or are exhibiting this pattern in recent races. These types of horses have shown a tendency for distributing most of their energy later in the race, the hallmark of success on the lawn.

Take a look at Theres No Tomorrow (page 126) in the eighth race at Bay Meadows on May 10, 2001, a maiden claimer at a mile on the turf. This filly had never been on the grass, but her final number progression as a four-year-old caught my eye. The improvement was incremental and steady, but more importantly, her last two route spreads were (-2) and (-7).

Before these last two races, she had only run one other negative dirt spread, that being the 58/61- reversal in March of her three-year-old season. She was obviously learning to distribute her energy later in the race, and with that profile and facing a weak field, I thought she had a reasonable chance in her initial grass foray. After lagging behind early, Theres No Tomorrow rallied to a $17.00 victory.

Unlike a dirt spread, a **turf spread** is a positive number when the final number is *higher* than the pace number. The turf spread is calculated by subtracting the pace number from the final number (final number minus pace number). If a horse's debut race was on the turf and it runs a turf spread of plus ten points (+10) or more while earning a competitive final number, give it serious consideration in its next grass attempt. Since grass races tend to go slower than dirt races in the early stages, this type of spread for a one-number turf horse is similar to a dirt compression line. Horses coming off these opening plus ten point or more turf spreads have demonstrated an affinity for the lawn, and often move up considerably next time out.

Cathode, Take My Note and Cherokee Kim (page 127) typify this look, and all three won their next race. Note that Cathode and Cherokee Kim had run dirt compression lines in their debuts, another signal they might like the turf.

In general, when evaluating lightly raced turf horses, give the edge to the contender with the best turf spread, all else being equal. In addition, if the early pace looks contentious, I might prefer a slower final number horse with a superior spread (56/70 over 65/71).

Another pattern to look for with youngsters is a gradual decline in turf pace numbers with relatively consistent final numbers. Although not as powerful as the TD line, the incremental improvement in finishing ability is a positive sign.

4TH 3AX MARCH 29 - 1 MILE TURF

	4		5		6	
D						
e			HO	=73-w	(69)=	
c			HO	66+　64	(70)	
N						
o						
v						
O			SA	=64+	(74)=	
c						
t			SA	=62-	(77)=	
S						
e			DM	=68"	(73)=	
P	DM	59　60 (62)	DM	=71+w	(73)=	
A	DM	=68　(68)=				
u						
g						
J			DM	=69-	(76)=	
u						
l			HO	=70"	(78)=	
J						
u			HO	=70-	(68)=	
n						
M			HO	=70+	(79)=	
a						
y						
A						
p						
r						
M					-->	
a						
r						
F						
e					SA	=^71-w　(64)=
b						
J						
a					SA	=70　(74)=
n						

EQUIFORM™ Pg: 16   **GUTHRUN (FR)   (118)**   THE XTRAS™

4TH SAX MARCH 29 - 1 MILE TURF

	2	3	4
D			
e			
c		GG =69+ (64)=	
N			
o			
v			
O			
c		SA =70-w (73)=	
t			
S			
e			
p		DM 66" 66(73)63	
A			
u			
g		DM =68" (57)=	
J			
u			
l			
J			
u		HO =71 (62)=	
n			
M			
a			
y			
A			
p			
r			
M			-->
a			
r			
F			
e			
b			SA =72- (74)=
J			
a			
n			SA =72" (66)=

EQUIFORM™ Pg: 19   **GLORIOUS LINDA (FR)   (120)**   THE XTRAS™

4TH SAX MARCH 29 - 1 MILE TURF

	5	6	7
D		SA =73-w (63)=	
e			
c		HO =71 (61)=	
N			
o			
v		SA =72- (64)=	
O			
c		SA =72+w (60)=	
t		SA =69+ (75)=	
S			
e			
p			
A			
u		DM =69- (66)=	
g		DM =70 (61)=	
J			
u			
l			
J			
u		HO =72- (60)=	
n			
M			
a			
y		HO =71- (61)=	
A		SA =71+ (73)=	
p	SA =71+w (62)=		
r			
M	SA =^72"w (66)=		-->
a			
r		SA =.73- (71)=	
	SA =71 (64)=		
F			
e			SA =^73-w (61)=
b	SA =^73- (61)=		
J			
a		SA =72- (65)=	
n			

EQUIFORM™ Pg: 77 **ELTAWAASUL (114)** THE XTRAS™

8TH FGX JANUARY 6 - 1 MILE ABOUT TURF

3	4	5

D
e
c
N
o
v
O
c
t
S
e
p
A
u
g
J
u
l
J
u
n
M
a
y
A
p
r
M
a
r
F
e
b
J
a
n

FG   =72+   (56) =

BE   =71"   (78) =

SR   =:72+   (64) =

BE   =74"   (70) =

MP   =72-   (65) =

-->

EQUIFORM™ Pg: 86   **NAT'S BIG PARTY**   **(117)**   THE XTRAS™

`8TH FGX JANUARY  6 - 1 MILE ABOUT TURF`

	5	6	7
D			
e			
c		FG =72	(51)=
N			
o	AQ =74+ (67)=		
v		AQ =70 (69)=	
O	AQ =73" (60)=		
c		BE =74- (55)=	
t			
S	BE =^76- (61)=		
e		ME =75-w (69)=	
p		SR =73 *(59)=*	
A	SR ^69" 66 (65)		
u		SR =:75- (57)=	
g	SR =75+ (64)=		
J			
u	BE =75w (60)=		
l	BE =74 (58)=		
J		BE =74" *(58)=*	
u	BE =73 (63)=	BE =72"w *(57)=*	
n		BE =70+ (61)=	
M	BE =73-w (60)=		
a	BE /69 67 (67)		
y			
A	AQ =73+w (66)=	AQ =72+ (61)=	
p			
r			
M			
a		GP =71" (50)=	
r			
F			
e		GP =74 (60)=	
b			
J		GP =70" (60)=	
a			
n			

-->

EQUIFORM™ Pg: 68   **AFTERNOON ROSE   (119)**
6TH GPI FEBRUARY 16 - 1 1/16 MILES ABOUT TURF

	2		3	
D CR	-66+w	(58) =		
e			-->	
b			GP -70	(62) -
J				

EQUIFORM™ Pg: 65   **TANALLOVER   (115)**
6TH GPI FEBRUARY 16 - 1 1/16 MILES ABOUT TURF

	2		3	
D CR	-64-	(70) -		
e				
c				
N CR	-^66-w	(77) -		
o				
v CR	-65-	(71) -		
O				
c				
t CN	-61+	(64) -		
S				
e CN	-65+	(74) -		
P				
A				
u LR	49+	(55) 64		
g				
J LR	57+	(62) 72		
u LR	48+	(55) 67		
e			-->	
b			GP -65-	(59) -
J				
a			GP -62-	(65) -

EQUIFORM™ Pg: 58   **WHERE'S CIELO**   (115)
6TH GDI FEBRUARY 16 - 1 1/16 MILES ABOUT TURF

	2		3	
D e c	CR -^65-	(62)-		
N o v	LR -67	(67)-		
O c t	CN 56" 58	(69) 69		
S e p	CN -^67-w	(54)-		
	DE -64	(60)-		
A u g				
J u l	LR 55+	(63) 73		
	LR 51+	(59) 66		
F e b			-->	
J a			GP -65+	(51)-
			GP -66"	(64)-

EQUIFORM™ Pg: 66   **CANDY MINT**   (117)
6TH GDI FEBRUARY 16 - 1 1/16 MILES ABOUT TURF

	2		3	
D e c	CR -^65	(64)-		
	CR 53+ 63	(71)		
N o v	CR -68"w	(68)-		
O c t	CR -69"	(62)-		
J	CR ^55-	(65) 74		
F e b			-->	
J			GP -69"	(51)-

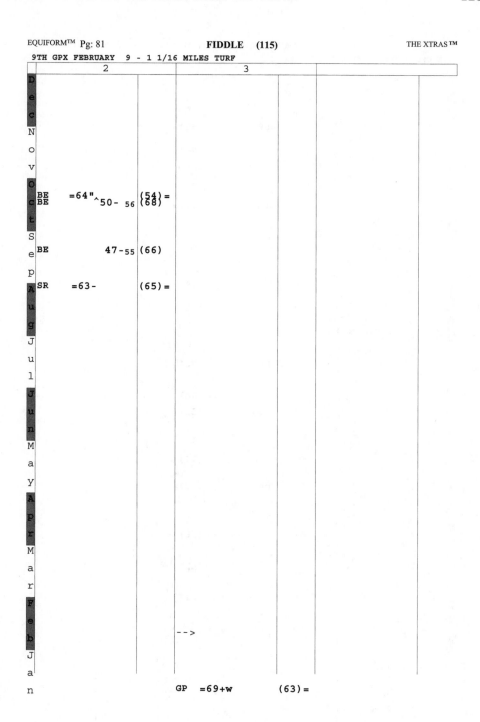

EQUIFORM™ Pg: 81 **FIDDLE** (115) THE XTRAS™

9TH GPX FEBRUARY   9 - 1 1/16 MILES TURF

	2	3			
D					
e					
c					
N					
o					
v					
O	BE =64"∧50- 56	{54} = {88}			
c	BE				
t					
S					
e	BE 47-55 (66)				
p					
A	SR =63- (65) =				
u					
g					
J					
u					
l					
J					
u					
n					
M					
a					
y					
A					
p					
r					
M					
a					
r					
F					
e					
b		-->			
J					
a					
n		GP =69+w (63) =			

EQUIFORM™ Pg: 62   **CASTLE COMER**   **(116)**   THE XTRAS™

9TH CRC DECEMBER 27 - 1 1/8 MILES TURF

D		2		3		
e				-->		
c						
N	AQ	52	56 (58)	CR =68"	(55) =	
o	ME	61-	58 (62)	CR =^67	(62) =	
v						
O						
c				CR =68-	(57) =	
t	ME	51	(61) 57			
S						
e						
p				CR =71+w	(58) =	
A				CR =^69-	(58) =	
u						
g						
J						
u				CR =^70+w	(66) =	
l						
J				CR ^60"	65 (70)	
u				CR =^68+	(55) =	
n						
M				GP =66-	(61) =	
a				GP =65	(60) =	
y						
A						
p				GP 53"	54 (58)	
r						
M				GP 58	55 (57)	
a				GP 58+	58 (62)	
r						
F				GP 65	59 (57)	
e						
b						
J						
a						
n				AQ 47- (56) 45		

EQUIFORM™ Pg: 78   **ANSWER TO ME   (114)**   THE XTRAS™

9TH CRC DECEMBER 31 - 1 1/16 MILES TURF

Month	2			3		
D	CR	64+w	(70)73	-->		
e						
c						
N				CR ^72w	65	(65)
o						
v						
O				CR =72-w		(68)=
c						
t				CR 70	66	(69)
S						
e	CR	/57"	(66)80			
P	CR	60- 62	(73)80	CR ^74+w	66	(70)
A						
u	CR	58"	(67)58	CR =66-		(50)=
g						
J				CR /68	66	(74)
u						
l						
J				CR =68"w		(65)=
u						
n				CR =64+		(62)=
M						
a				GP =71"		(61)=
y				GP 62+		(71)60
A				GP 62		(72)79
p						
r						
M						
a						
r						
F						
e				GP 55-		(71)78
b						
J						
a						
n						

EQUIFORM™ Pg: 43 **THERES NO TOMORROW   (123)** THE XTRAS™

8TH RACE BM MAY 10TH   - 1 MILE TURF - Three Year Olds 115 lbs.

Month	2	3	4
D		GG 61- (65)$_{65}$	
e		GG 64 (69)$_{65}$	
c	GG 56- (58)$_{57}$		
N			
o		GG 57" (65)$_{58}$	
v			
O			
c		BM 57" (62)$_{61}$	
t			
S			
e			
p			
A			
u			
g			
J			
u			
l			
J			
u			
n			
M			
a		-->	
y			
A			BM 65 $_{59}$(58)
p		GG 63+ (64)$_{66}$	BM 64" $_{57}$(62)
r		BM 61- $_{56}$(58)	GG 63 (68)$_{66}$
M			
a		BM /56" $_{56}$(61)	GG 63+ (69)$_{66}$
r			
F		BM /57 $_{58}$(64)	GG 62" (67)$_{60}$
e			
b		BM >59 (65)$_{67}$	GG >61- (70)$_{69}$
J			
a		GG 65- (65)$_{66}$	
n			

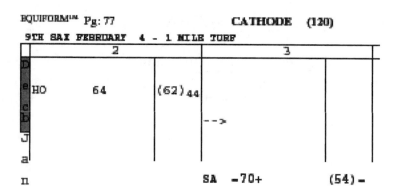

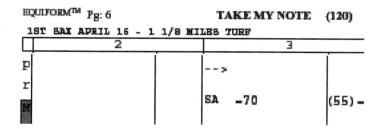

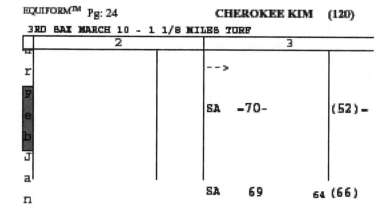

Surface Return or Resurface

Dirt to turf is a different story than first time turf. This situation arises when a horse has already had one or more grass races and is returning to the turf after racing on the dirt. If a horse's initial effort(s) on the turf were substandard (lower than his usual dirt numbers), look to see if its recent dirt spreads have tightened (or reversed) in the interim. Look for the same pattern with horses that have run well previously on the turf and are now returning after a sequence of dirt races.

Straight A Student (page 135) entered in the fourth race at Hialeah Park on March 31, 2001, illustrates the concept. His last four dirt spreads leading into the upcoming grass race were 1, -2, -5, and -12. With proven back turf ability, and picture perfect conditioning, Straight A Student rolled home at $7.40.

If it looks like a horse prefers grass and is returning to that surface, a new pace top on the dirt preceding the surface switch is powerful. By running well early on a surface that is not its favorite, the horse will usually respond favorably when placed back on the grass.

Dyna's Club (page 136) had shown a preference for the grass right from the start. Her first try on the surface came after a 3-point final top of 72+ on the dirt. We would expect a reasonable bounce off that effort, but the fact that she ran a 72- in her initial turf attempt was the first sign that this might be her preferred surface. When placed in a turf route in her next start, she ran a 75+.

For some reason, Dyna's Club began her 4yo season on the dirt, and turned in two weak efforts. But in her next six races, all on the grass, she ran 72-74 finals, again demonstrating she relished the turf. In her first two races of 2001, she caught good and yielding turf courses, something she had yet to encounter, and ran weak races against graded stakes company. Had she lost her good form, had the competition been too tough, or were the off turf courses the culprit? The dirt sprint on February 24th provided the answer for Equiform users regarding her current condition. The new dirt pace top (80) signaled this mare was ready for a peak effort. When placed back on her favored surface by trainer Ron Ellis (11/35 at the meet), jockey Chris McCarron gave her a masterful front-end ride, winning a head bob at $16.40 while earning a 74".

After two dull races on the dirt to begin her career, Soixante Dix (page 137) improved eight points to a 65 when first placed on the grass. Trainer James Toner left her in New York for the winter, and Soixante Dix worked her way up to a 64-3/4 on the dirt, while tightening her spreads (12, 11, 1, 0). This was ideal preparation for a return to her preferred surface. On April 21, 2001, Toner placed her in a $35,000 claimer on the Aqueduct turf and she responded with a 69, paying $34.80.

Another powerful dirt to turf angle involves a horse that runs a dirt reversal immediately preceding the turf race. This applies to both first-time grass horses and horses returning to the turf. For a dramatic illustration of this concept, look at the 9th race at the Fairgrounds on March 26, 2001. The three betting favorites were Sarah Lane's Oates (6/5), Marie's Star (2/1), and Another Grey Lady (5/1) (pages 138–140). The favorite had tailed off in her last three races and was coming off a seven-week layoff. Marie's Star hadn't been on the grass in over two years, had never hit the board in three previous grass attempts and had weak turf breeding. Another Grey Lady had run a 72- grass final at Louisiana Downs the previous September, but hadn't gotten back to that figure in her last six races. None of the top three choices exhibited any positive conditioning patterns.

Now look at Sparkles of Luck (page 141). She had peaked with a 71+ at Lone Star in May 2000, and hung the first defeat on the much ballyhooed Hallowed Dreams in August. Her two previous turf efforts had been acceptable. In fact, her first time on the surface, she earned a 68", better than she had ever run on the dirt at that point. After the Hallowed Dreams race, she was laid off for over three months. She ran a cyclical pace top on February 15, 2001, and then came the key race, a dirt reversal to a 68+. This late distribution of energy was the ideal prep for a return to the grass. It appeared that a 71 or 72 final number would give her a chance, and the reversal suggested that Sparkles of Luck was likely to get back to that area now. Even though she was four pounds overweight at 114, she was still in receipt of 1.6 points from Sarah Lane's Oates at 122. I made her true chances around 10/1, and when I made my wagers at a minute to post (which is more like four minutes at the Fairgrounds), she was 35/1 and rising. In addition to a win/place bet, I boxed her with the favorite in the exacta, and played a trifecta rundown combining these two in the first and second slots with the whole field.

My confidence in the play was shaken a bit when Sparkles of Luck broke through the gate before the start. But after being collared, she calmly reloaded, and with a ground-saving trip from Gerald Melancon, got the jump on the fast-closing Sarah Lane's Oates to win by a nostril at 44/1. The exacta came back $286 and the trifecta $8,611 when a long shot ran third.

Although we discussed some turf to dirt angles in the General Principles chapter, here is one that combines a turf pace low with a return to the main track.

Look at El Nativo's last race as a 3 year old (page 142), where he ran a turf pace low coupled with a lifetime best 22-point turf spread. Entered in a dirt route at Santa Anita on February 1, 2001, and making his third start off an eight-month layoff, El Nativo was primed for a top effort. He had run a 68" on the main track earlier in his career, which compared favorably with the turf numbers he was running at that time, so he rated to transfer his current good form to the dirt without a hitch. At 11/1, he was a solid wager and returned $24.00.

After beginning his career with two compression lines, Lucount (page 143) threw in a clunker in the mud. He began his three year-old season with two more dirt races, getting to a 63 final top in February. Placed on the grass for his next two starts, Lucount ran a 63/66- and 44/63. Though not a TD line, the 19-point spread in his last race to a turf pace low was encouraging. Also, Lucount was not bred that well for the turf, so he figured to run better than a 66- on the dirt (always keep these preferences in mind when evaluating surface switches with lightly raced horses).

On May 31, 2001 at Belmont Park, Lucount was entered in a 1-1/16 mile dirt race for maiden claimers. The deserving although overbet favorite in the race was Freddy's Dream (page 144) at even money. In addition to his concealed conditioning, Lucount was dropping from a maiden special weight race, had some bullet dirt drills sprinkled in his workout line, and figured to be a good price. Freddy's Dream was running in the 67 area, and I felt Lucount had a chance to reach that number in this race. A few minutes to post Lucount's odds were 20/1 and climbing. Then, I realized who the trainer was – John P Campo Jr, who was 1 for 51 on the year. All of sudden, I got cold feet, and second-guessed my analysis. I just couldn't bring myself to bet such a plodder in a maiden claimer with a trainer mired in a long drought. Even though I knew Lucount was in decent form, I passed the race.

When the gates opened, Freddy's Dream ducked inward and careened into the rail, losing all chance, while Lucount contested the early pace and dug in resolutely in the stretch to win at 36/1. This is the kind of surprise that reminds one that, for the most part, horses win races - not jockeys or trainers or tips or statistics. If I didn't know Campo Jr was the trainer, I would have made this horse 6/1 based on his raw ability. Even knowing that Campo Jr was the trainer, I should have made him 12/1 or so.

Had he broken cleanly, Freddy's Dream may very well have won the race (he finished fourth, beaten six lengths). But the gods were smiling on Lucount this day, and only after the race did I glance at some trainer statistics. Over the last couple of years, Campo Jr was 4/24 or 17% with the turf to dirt move, which was much better than his overall win percentage. I took the rest of the day off.

Coming off a new pace top on January 11, 2001, Ragtime Tune (page 145) exploded to a 66 in her first route attempt. She then bounced to a 63", and after a couple of brief layoffs tried grass for the first time on April 27, running a 65/63". In her next start, she showed good condition by running a 53/63", creating a TD line. Placed back on the dirt on May 25, she rated to move back toward her 66 dirt top. She only ran a 64-3/4, but still prevailed returning $16.80.

Now that we know the patterns that predict improved grass performance, we would like to expound on some other observations concerning turf racing.

First of all, horses tend to "bounce" less violently off big grass efforts. The fact that turf horses distribute their energy more evenly, coupled with the more forgiving nature of the surface (less concussive strain), allows them to run more consistent final numbers. The corollary to this phenomenon is that the conservation of energy makes for more clustered finishes. Accordingly, a big edge in final numbers is more significant on the turf. A horse with a two point final number advantage on the dirt is not as formidable as a horse with the same advantage on the turf.

As we do not normalize pace numbers, turf marathons can often produce very low pace numbers. When evaluating a TPL or a TD line, be cognizant of this, and be sure to base your analysis on races run at similar distances (an 1/8th of a mile or less of each other). The same holds true for horses that have a mix of turf routes and sprints. Compare only the route races in the sequence (note - we treat 7 and 7-1/2 furlong turf races around two turns as routes). Also remember that when evaluating dirt pace tops and turf pace lows, only compare pace numbers on each specific surface (dirt vs. dirt and turf vs. turf).

Turf sprints can be quite daunting for many figure handicappers, but we have found them to offer some good opportunities if certain precepts are followed. The key is to identify what profiles are winning at a particular track. Then look for patterns on The Xtras that typify these profiles.

A pronounced final number edge is certainly worth playing at the right price, but more often, the value is to be found elsewhere. The 5-1/2 furlong races at Hollywood Park sometimes favor early speed, especially when the course gets very dry. In this case, a new pace top on the turf can be a positive sign. The about 6-1/2 furlong turf races at Santa Anita are another matter. Here, the unique configuration of the course favors horses that have already negotiated it successfully and/or mid-post routers with competitive final numbers on TD lines.

Although most figure makers utilize the projection method in "creating" their figures, Equiform parts company with this dubious practice. Its practitioners are often forced to "fudge" their final numbers due to the influence of pace.

As an example, on September 9, 2000, two turf races were run over the Belmont inner turf course, one a NW1 allowance race, the other the Grade I Man O'War Stakes. In the allowance race, I was fortunate enough to back Understood, who paid $64 after being awarded first place on a disqualification. The fractions for that 1-1/4 mile race were 23.66, 48.29, 1:13.78, 1:39.08 and 2:04.28. The Man O'War, run a few races later at 1-3/8 miles, went in 25.54, 50.94, 1:16.14, 1:41.04, 2:05.47, and 2:17.44. Formal Consent, the disqualified top horse in the allowance race earned a Beyer figure of 91, while the winner of the stakes race, Fantastic Light, was rewarded with a 106. The relationship of these final numbers makes no sense.

Although running his final eighth of a mile in a shade under 12 seconds, Fantastic Light was a head behind the leader's ten-furlong split of 2:05:47. Formal Consent ran the same ten furlongs in 2:04.28, and a horse of his caliber would usually require about 13 seconds to negotiate an extra eighth of a mile at this particular turf distance, for roughly the same final time as Fantastic Light. On The Xtras, Fantastic Light earned a 43/76- and Formal Consent a 51/74". On a final number basis, they ran about the same race, with most of the difference due to Fantastic Light carrying 126 pounds versus 121 for Formal Consent (remember, 5 pounds = 1 final number point).

As Beyer does not incorporate weight into his numbers, the 15-point difference between the final numbers is even more egregious. I have witnessed the same projection methods in operation with the turf figures of other services. As best as I can determine, the rationale for this practice is that they just can't fathom giving a NW1 allowance horse the same figure as a Grade I Stakes horse. They know the stakes horse is better, but their only recourse is the final number. At Equiform we have no such inhibitions or limitations. The distribution between the pace and final numbers solves the mystery.

I have no doubt that Fantastic Light would demolish Formal Consent in a turf marathon. Not because his final number is better, but rather that he ran a 33 point spread between his pace and final number compared to 23 for Formal Consent. Fantastic Light has demonstrated a sizable edge in finishing ability, and that is usually decisive in marathon grass races. In fact, at 1-1/4 miles and up on the grass, always give consideration to the horses with the best turf spreads even if their final numbers look a little light, as the final numbers are often just a function of the pace.

On February 9, 2001, two races were run at one mile over the Santa Anita turf course. The first race went 48.88 for the half with a final time of 1:34.97. The second one went in 45.92 and 1:35.13. The winner of the first one carried one pound less in weight. As Maxwell Smart used to say, would you believe that the winner of the first race received a Beyer figure 18 points higher than the winner of the second race? No, we find that hard to believe. How about 12 points? No, we find that hard to believe. How about 10 points since the winner was Hawksley Hill, who once almost won the Breeders Cup Mile? We don't think so.

What we do think is that due to the very slow pace in the first race, the Beyer figures in that event were inflated. Thus, the 18 point differential. On The Xtras, Hawksley Hill ran a 58/74 and Dr Park, the winner of the second one-mile turf race, ran a 78/74-. On a final number basis, they ran about the same, but the turf spreads (-4 for Dr Park and +16 for Hawksley Hill) varied dramatically. Hey Chief, I think Control should start using The Xtras. By the way, Chief, what are The Xtras?

Lest you think this projection business is limited to turf races, think again. As a poignant example, consider the 1989 Forego Handicap. Defending champion Quick Call (a noted Saratoga horse for the course), with Pat Day at the controls, was allowed to set a dawdling pace of 47 and change for the first half mile. There were some good sprinters behind him, and though they flew home, they could not catch the Spa specialist.

Mark Hopkins, then doing the Beyer numbers for the major New York tracks, wrote an article in the *Racing Form* regarding the difficulty he had in assigning a figure for the race. If he took the final time at face value, and gave it the same variant as the other sprints, he would have given Grade 2 stakes horses, that frequently earned triple digit Beyers, figures in the low 90's. It didn't "feel" right to him, so he made a separate variant for the Forego, thus inflating the final numbers 10 points or so. If ever there was a case where pace made the race, this was it, even though it was a premier event at venerable Saratoga.

Equiform has no need to make such "guesses". We report what actually occurred and let the distribution between the pace and final numbers tell the story.

EQUIFORM™ Pg: 56   **STRAIGHT A STUDENT (119)**   THE XTRAS™

8TH HIA APRIL 16 - 1 1/8 MILES TURF

	3	4	5
D			
e		CR 65+ 63(66)	
c			
N			
o			
v			
O			
c			
t			
S			
e		DE 71- 66(66)	
p			
A			
u			
g		DE =.73 (54)=	
J		DE =69+ (53)=	
u			
l			
J			
u		DE =73-w (65)=	
n		DE =71- (60)=	
M		DE /67+ 72(79)	
a			
y		DE 67- 62(62)	
A			
p			-->
r	HI 63 65(68)67	TA =67" (59)=	
M	TA 64"w (65)56	TA 69-w 61(61)	HI =^71"w ()=
a			
r		TA 67+ (74)66	
F	GP 61 60(62)		
e			GP 70 61(58)
b			GP ^66" 58(61)
J			
a			
n			GP 62" 59(60)

EQUIFORM™ Pg: 58   **DYNA'S CLUB**   (118)   THE XTRAS™

7TH SAX MARCH 16 - 1 MILE TURF

Month	3	4	5
Dec			
Nov		HO =73+ (69)=	
Nov		HO =74" (72)=	
Oct	SA =75+ (72)=		
Oct	SA =72- (74)=	SA =73- (73)=	
Sep	EM 72+ 70(74)		
Aug		DM =72+ (68)=	
Aug	EM 69+ 62(65)	DM =73+ (70)=	
Aug	EM >66+ 65(69)		
Jul		DM =73+w (70)=	
Jul	EM 66+ 67(75)		
Jun	EM 69+w 68(70)67	HO 67+ 66(72)69	
May	EM 68-w (74)75		
May	EM 68 68(75)79	HO 65" (69)57	
Apr	EM *60+* *(59)*50		
Mar			-->
Feb			SA >73- 73(80)78
Feb			GG =.72 (67)
Jan			SA =^70" (66)

EQUIFORM™ Pg: 25   **SOIXANTE DIX**   **(117)**   THE XTRAS™

4TH AQU APRIL 21 - 1 MILE TURF

	2		3		
D					
e					
c					
N					
o					
v					
O					
c	BE	=65	(62)=		
t	BE	57- 60	(72) 77		
S					
e					
p					
A	SR	57"	(61) 71		
u					
g					
J					
u					
l					
J					
u					
n					
M					
a					
y					
A					
p			-->		
r					
M			AQ /65-w	(65) 62	
a					
r					
F			**AQ 61- 57**	**(62)**	
e					
b			AQ 58-	(69) 69	
J			AQ 59+	(71) 69	
a					
n					

EQUIFORM™ Pg: 89　　　　　　**SARAH LANE'S OATES　(122)**　　　　THE XTRAS™

9TH FGX MARCH 26　　　STATE-BRED - 1 MILE ABOUT TURF

	5			6		7	
D				FG　=^70-	(65)=		
e							
c	FG　=71+	(62)=	FG　=74w	(75)=		
N	FG　71"	64 (66)	FG　=70+	(57)=		
o						
v						
O	LD　=72-w	(58)=	LD　=73"	(61)=		
c						
t						
S	LD　=72+	(59)=				
e	LD　=72+	(57)=	LD　=74-w	(62)=		
p			LD　=74-	(61)=		
A						
u						
g						
J			LD　=73+	(59)=		
u						
l	LD　=70+	(57)=	LD　=74+w	(63)=		
J						
u						
n						
M	LS　=:71+	(58)=	LS　=71"	(53)=		
a						
y	LS　=70+	(56)=				
A						
p	LS　=72	(55)=	LS　=75"w	(72)=		
r						
M	FG　=73-w	(61)=	FG　=73w	(68)= -->		
a						
r	FG　=71	(53)=	FG　=72+	(61)=		
F			FG　=72"w	(61)=		
e						
b	FG　=^73+	()=			FG　=72+	(69)
J						
a	FG　=73+w	(61)=	FG　=71-	(52)=	FG　=71	(63)
n	FG　=^73"	(61)=				

EQUIFORM™ Pg: 88   **MARIE'S STAR   (113)**   THE XTRAS™

9TH FGX MARCH 26   STATE-BRED - 1 MILE ABOUT TURF

5	6	7
	CD /69+ $_{67}$ (72) $_{74}$	
	EP 69" $_{67}$ (72)	
	CD 71w $_{67}$ (70)	
	CD 72w $_{70}$ (78)	
	KE 71w $_{70}$ (73) $_{72}$	
		-->
	FG 70+ (73) $_{77}$	FG /69"w $_{65}$ (71)
	FG 68-w (70) $_{73}$	
	FG 63"w (67) $_{69}$	
	FG 64+ (68) $_{70}$	
	FG /67- (64) $_{63}$	
		FG ^68+w (68) $_{64}$
	FG 66+ (67) $_{73}$	

D e c N o v O c t S e p A u g J u l J u n M a y A p r M a r F e b J a n

EQUIFORM™ Pg: 87   **ANOTHER GREY LADY**   (116)   THE XTRAS™

9TH FGX MARCH 26   STATE-BRED - 1 MILE ABOUT TURF

	3	4	5
Dec	FG 66- 66 (72)	FG 68" 68 (71)	
Nov	FG 64+ 68 (77)		
Nov	LD 70-w 68 (76)		
Oct	LD =67w (73)=	LD 70- 69 (71)	
Sep	LD 58+ (70)77	LD =67- (67)=	
Sep		LD =72- (70)=	
Sep	LD 54" (72)78		
Aug	LD 57" (73)79		
Aug		LD =71-w (71)=	
Aug	LD 59 64 (77)79		
Jul	LD 56+ (72)81	LD 69 70 (80)	
Jul	LD 54" (66)76	LD 70" 71 (74)72	
Jul	LD 59+ (74)82	LD =68"w (67)=	
Jun			
May		EV 63" 65 (71)	
Apr		EV 68+ (78)74	
Mar		FG =69" (71)=	-->
Mar		FG ^69-w 61 (65)	
Mar		FG 67- (64)61	FG /68+ 66 (73)
Feb		FG 69w 64 (69)	
Feb		FG 66" 63 (69)	FG 66+ (73)76
Jan	HU 61 (66)64	FG =67" (65)=	FG =70+w (69)

EQUIFORM™ Pg: 90   **SPARKLES OF LUCK (110)**   THE XTRAS™

9TH FGX MARCH 26   STATE-BRED - 1 MILE ABOUT TURF

Month	2	3	4
Dec		FG /66+ $(77)_{80}$	
Dec		FG =67" $()=$	
Nov		FG ^62 $(75)_{81}$	
Aug		EV 70-w $(87)_{96}$	
Jul		LD 67 $(78)_{82}$	
Jul		LS 67- $_{69}$ $(80)_{81}$	
Jun	*EV 58-* $(66)_{79}$		
May	*EV 64-* $(67)_{77}$	LS 71+ $(83)_{85}$	
May		LS =68" $(65)=$	
Apr		**LS 67-w** $()$	
Mar		FG 67" $(78)_{90}$ -->	
Mar		FG 67" $(76)_{80}$	
Feb			**FG /68+** $_{64}$ **(67)**
Feb		FG 66" $(78)_{84}$	
Feb			FG 64 $(78)_{85}$
Jan		FG ^68-w $(72)_{72}$	

EQUIFORM™ Pg: 27　　　　　　　**EL NATIVO　(117)**　　　　　　THE XTRAS™

4TH SAX FEBRUARY　1 - 1 MILE DIRT

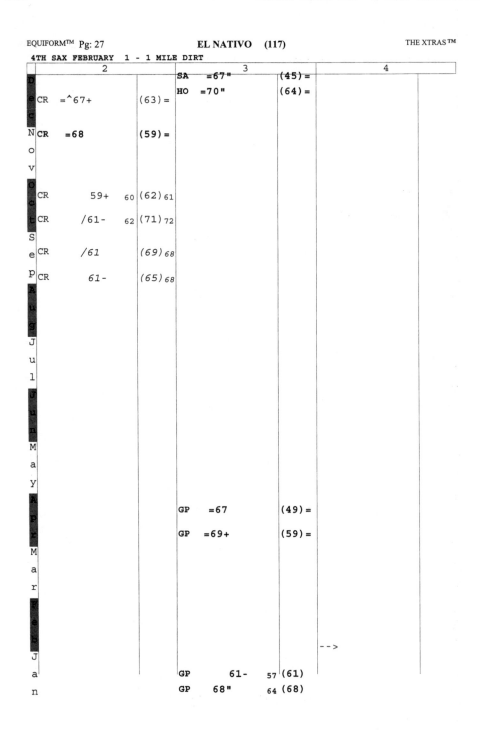

	2		3		4
D			SA　=67"	(45)=	
e	CR　=^67+	(63)=	HO　=70"	(64)=	
c					
N	CR　=68	(59)=			
o					
v					
O	CR　　59+	60 (62) 61			
c	CR　　/61-	62 (71) 72			
t					
S	CR　　/61	(69) 68			
e					
P	CR　　61-	(65) 68			
A					
u					
g					
J					
u					
l					
J					
u					
n					
M					
a					
y					
A			GP　=67	(49)=	
p			GP　=69+	(59)=	
r					
M					
a					
r					
F					
e					
b					-->
J					
a			GP　　61-	57 (61)	
n			GP　　68"	64 (68)	

EQUIFORM™ Pg: 11   **LUCOUNT** **(117)**   THE XTRAS™

2ND BEL MAY 31 - 1 1/16 MILES DIRT

	2		3	
D				
e				
c				
N	AQ \53	58 (61)		
o				
v				
O	AQ 62"	61 (65)		
c				
t	BE 60-	60 (60)		
S				
e				
p				
A				
u				
g				
J				
u				
l				
J				
u				
n				
M			-->	
a			BE *=63*	*(44)* =
y				
A			AQ =66-	(63) =
p				
r				
M				
a				
r				
F			AQ 63	58 (59)
e				
b				
J				
a				
n			AQ 60-	50 (50)

EQUIFORM™ Pg: 9 **FREDDY'S DREAM (117)** THE XTRAS™

2ND BEL MAY 31 - 1 1/16 MILES DIRT

	2	3		
D e c				
N o v	CD 62 $_{59}$(69) $_{74}$			
O c t				
S e p				
A u g	SR \54" (68) $_{74}$			
J u l				
J u n				
M a y		-->		
		BE 67 $_{64}$(68)		
A p r		AQ 66" $_{65}$(64)		
M a r		HI =63+ () =		
F e b		GP =64+ (63) =		
J a n				

EQUIFORM™ Pg: 10   **RAGTIME TUNE (118)**   THE XTRAS™

2ND BEL MAY 25 - 1 MILE DIRT

	2	3	
D	AQ 57+	(68) 70	
e			
c			
N			
o			
v			
O			
c			
t			
S			
e			
p			
A			
u			
g			
J			
u			
l			
J			
u			
n			
M		-->	
a		BE =63"	(53) =
y			
A		AQ =63"	(65) =
p			
r			
M		AQ 51" 58	(69)
a			
r			
F			
e			
b		AQ 63" 61	(65)
J		AQ 66w 63	(70)
a			
n		AQ 58	(73) 77

Chapter 11

Track Biases

Track bias is a very real but elusive phenomenon that is difficult to quantify. Although we make no up-front adjustments in our numbers for bias, it is sometimes necessary to factor in past biases to get a complete and accurate picture of a horse's current form cycle.

Once viewed as a rather arcane concept, track bias is now embraced as a key handicapping factor. However, the determination of real track biases is more art than science, and it is not uncommon for different observers to draw different conclusions regarding the nature of a particular day's racing surface. Is the inside really good, or were those early rail-skimming winners just the best horses in their respective races? Is the track favoring speed, or did the frontrunners enjoy uncontested early leads?

Many players assume that because a horse ran a creditable race against the bias in its last start, its chances should be upgraded in its next race. This is not always prudent. For example, if a horse runs a top effort against the bias, it is in effect a bigger top, and could set the horse back for a while. Conversely, running a top effort with the bias may not take too much out of the horse. Trying to quantify the precise effect of biases is problematical, but give it consideration in your analysis. We are fond of horses which run new pace tops against the bias when accompanied by a low final number. They often return to run well in their next start at overlaid odds.

Proper determination of track bias requires excellent handicapping skills. Although some track programs, recap shows, public handicappers, and the *Racing Form Charts Weekly* all offer some guidance, nothing substitutes for intense personal observation and analysis.

The ability to detect a bias on race day is a potent weapon. Past biases can assist the handicapper in evaluating a horse's previous efforts and relating them to its current form cycle. But only by identifying biases in real time can the player reap the greatest benefits.

As I prepared to tackle the December 29, 2000 card at Aqueduct, I noted that the previous day had seemed to favor outside closers and stalkers. Although biases can disappear quickly, I was on the alert to see if the previous day's trend would continue. The first race at six furlongs was a wide-open affair, and the first three finishers all came from off the pace. The second race, a route, was won wire to wire. But the third race left me thinking the outside closing bias was still operative in sprints. The 8/5 favorite, Rhythmical Lady, got to the top, but couldn't withstand the late charge of We're Jamin (page 151) at 14/1. Right behind the top two were two other closers, with 67/1 Judge Carrie a close-up fourth.

As an aside, I had We're Jamin due to the BPP's (back past performances). As the *Racing Form* only provides the past performances for the last ten races (twelve at premier tracks), races that occurred before then are hidden from the public. Yes, *Racing Form* users can scan the career box to see the best Beyer at the distance, but that figure could have been earned at any track and at any point in the horse's development. We're Jamin had run a competitive sprint number at Aqueduct just before the Form's twelve race cutoff. She also was an outside closer, nicely fitting the current profile of the track. She paid $30.00.

In the next race, another sprint, Jessica Rapid (page 152) had the preferred look. After a new pace top in early October, she won off the double delay (two intervening turf races) at 11/1. In that win, she ran a (-8) dirt spread, the type of late distribution that should help her take advantage of the prevailing bias on December 29. Well back in the early going, Jessica Rapid rallied wide to score at 8/1.

The fall and spring Keeneland meets are both only three weeks long, but usually provide great plays for handicappers armed with

EQUIFORM pace numbers. The Keeneland dirt surface can become extremely biased towards inside speed. On those occasions, top final figure horses that lack competitive early pace are often left in the dust at short odds. The ability to get to the lead on the rail is crucial. Otherwise ordinary horses able to secure that position can turn into world-beaters. By looking at the two furlong numbers in conjunction with the pace number, one can cash some nice tickets.

The second race at Keeneland on April 12, 2001 demonstrates the principle (see page 153). A field of ten maiden fillies faced the starter. Wilderness Storm, the 6/5 favorite, had an (81) pace number along with a 93 two furlong number, and was on obvious threat. Although Paris Lady had run big pace numbers (82 and 86) in her two 3yo races, she did not exhibit the same early lick in her 4yo debut. All but two horses had earned a better final number than Janet's Cat, but her early speed, coupled with a new pace top, made her worth a second look. Her (82) pace number was best except for Paris Lady, and in the two furlong department, her 89 trailed only Wilderness Storm. If Wilderness Storm faltered, Janet's Cat had a chance to make the lead, and when I saw 40/1 on the board, I couldn't resist. When Wilderness Storm bobbled at the break, half the battle was over. Janet's Cat sped to a 2-1/2 length lead after a quarter mile and won the race by 3-3/4 lengths, returning $100.20.

The very next day, the bias looked even stronger. I got shut out of a win bet on Apalachee Island in the first race at a mile and a sixteenth. After sitting second behind the 9/5 favorite Dark Guest, he moved to the lead on the inside after three quarters. When passed by rallying Schizophrenic in mid-stretch, I was glad I got shutout, but only momentarily. Apalachee Island fought back on the inside, regained the lead, and went on to win by a neck at 10/1.

The Xtras for the major contenders in the second race are presented on pages 154–157. In this race at 6-1/2 furlongs, Casanova Consort (2/1) and Tricky Sis (5/2) were the two favorites. Although Casanova Consort was coming off a dirt top, I still respected her good early speed and inside post. Horses coming off tops often don't bounce much when they catch a bias or an off surface that suits them. Tricky Sis and Dancin B B (9/2) were both closers unsuited to the prevailing bias.

Now look at Axe N Ice. After a peak effort of 69+ on December 27, she was making her third start after a brief layoff. She had run an (80) pace number over this same Keeneland surface a year earlier, and the (77) pace number in her last start hinted she might be coming around. What sold me on her was the 68 turnback number she earned in that last start while beaten almost eighteen lengths. She had concealed final number power, the requisite early pace ability and, best of all, was flashing at 10/1 on the tote. Axe N Ice spurted to lead from her outside post, shook off early pressure from Casanova Consort, and after being collared by Day After at the sixteenth pole, dug in on the inside to win by a $\frac{1}{2}$ length, returning $21.40.

I can count on one hand the number of times I have witnessed back to back races captured by horses that lost the lead in mid-stretch, and then re-rallied to win. Most of the fingers belong to Keeneland.

The following day, April 14, 2001, featured the Blue Grass Stakes, and the best pace number horses, Millennium Wind and Songanda-prayer ran one-two around the track. Earlier on the card, I had found another nice play in the fifth race. In that event at six furlongs, Sams Tune was the even money favorite by virtue of her consistent big Beyer numbers. Sams Tune also had decent pace ability, but when I took a closer look at City Fair, my course was clear (pages 158–159). City Fair had run (80) and (86) pace numbers during the previous Keeneland meet along with an 84 two furlong number. She rated to get to the top in this event, and with a buried 71 turnback number plus a big jockey switch to Jerry Bailey, I couldn't believe I was getting 5/1 as they loaded into the gate. Bailey did get her to the front, but was caught by Pine For Me at the eighth pole. However, the bias was still in full force, and City Fair, under Bailey's vigorous urging, fought back to win by a length.

In summary, when after a comprehensive analysis you suspect a strong bias, get on board. Have the courage to bet horses that fit the winning profile over fast final figure horses. You will be surprised how much money you can make riding just a two or three day wave.

EQUIFORM™ Pg: 29   **WE'RE JAMIN (119)**   THE XTRAS™

3RD AQU DECEMBER 29 - 6 FURLONGS INNER DIRT

	2	3	4
			-->
Dec	ME 69-w (74)$_{80}$		
Nov			
			ME 65″ $_{67}$ (75)
Oct			ME 59 (68)$_{72}$
Sep			**ME =63+ (58)**
			MP 65- (75)$_{81}$
Aug			MP ^67 (79)$_{74}$
Jul		MP 71w (81)$_{77}$	
		MP 64 $_{67}$ (79)	MP 63+ (74)$_{71}$
Jun		MP 65″w (78)$_{80}$	MP 62+ (75)$_{81}$
		MP 65+ (71)$_{72}$	
May			
Apr			
Mar		**AQ 67″ $_{67}$ (71)**	
		AQ 67 $_{70}$ (69)	
Feb		AQ 68 (68)$_{80}$	
Jan		AQ 59+ (70)$_{80}$	

EQUIFORM™ Pg: 36   **JESSICA RAPID   (114*)**   THE XTRAS™

4TH AQU DECEMBER 29 STATE-BRED - 6 FURLONGS INNER DIRT

Dec	2			3		
D	AQ	53	54 (55)	-->		
e	AQ	\54"	51 (51)			
c				AQ	67-w	60 (59)
N						
o						
v				AQ	=64"	(61)=
O						
c				BE	=68-	(52)=
t				BE	65"	68 (74)
S				BE	61	55 (58)
e						
p				SR	=65	(55)=
A						
u				SR	/62-	65 (73)
g						
J				BE	67	65 (73)
u						
l				BE	=64-	(56)=
J				BE	=:68	(48)=
u						
n				BE	64"	62 (69)
M				BE	51-	58 (65)
a						
y				AQ	=^64-	(63)=
A						
p						
r				AQ	57	58 (63)
M				AQ	57-	57 (68)
a				AQ	61-	59 (64)
r				AQ	61"	54 (59)
F						
e				AQ	57-	60 (65)
b						
J						
a				AQ	57+	56 (63)
n						

EQUIFORM™ Pg: 13   **WILDERNESS STORM** (121)   THE XTRAS™

2ND KEE APRIL 12 - 6 FURLONGS DIRT

	2		3		4	
J r M a r F e b J	WO 59"	(68) 73				
					-->	
					PG 68	(81) 93
					PG -66	() -

EQUIFORM™ Pg: 14   **PARIS LADY** (121)   THE XTRAS™

2ND KEE APRIL 12 - 6 FURLONGS DIRT

	2		3		4	
M a Y A p r M a			AP 63	(82) 87		
			KE 63	68 (86) 89		
					-->	
					PG 67"	(72) 81

EQUIFORM™ Pg: 15   **JANET'S CAT** (121)   THE XTRAS™

2ND KEE APRIL 12 - 6 FURLONGS DIRT

	2		3		4	
r M a r F e					-->	
					TP 63	(82) 89
					TP 60+	(78) 79
					TP 59-	(69) 63

EQUIFORM™ Pg: 1   **CASANOVA CONSORT**   THE XTRAS™

	2		3		4	
D e c						
N o	CR =^67	(66)=	CD =68	(71)=		
v O	CR 63"w	60 (65)	CD =63"	(66)=		
c t						
S e	BE =67"	(66)=				
p **A**						
u	SR 60"	62 (73) 73	SR =66-	(65)=		
g **J**						
u	MP 58"	(68) 75				
l J						
u	CD 57+	(63) 79				
n **M**	CD 59"	(71) 71				
a y **A**						
p r			-->			
M a					TP 69"w	69 (79) 79
r			GP =58"	(58)=	TP 57-	(70) 66
F e						
b			GP =69+	(55)=	TP /50+	(68) 66
J					TP \66w	(72) 59
a n			GP =66"	(57)=		

EQUIFORM™ Pg: 2   **TRICKY SIS**   THE XTRAS™

Month	2	3	4
Dec		**TP** 56- 60 **(75)**	
Nov		TP /68w (71)55	
Oct		CD 62" (71)67	
Sep		TP 67- (73)64	
		TP 64-w 63 (75)77	
		TP 64- (76)84	
Aug			
Jul	SR 54+ (60)79		
	EP 60+ (70)74	CD 63" (73)79	
Jun			
May		CD 63- (75)82	
		CD 63" 62 (72)79	
Apr			-->
Mar		TP 65- (68)72	
			TP 67- (73)68
Feb			TP 68"w 67 (71)67
			TP /66+w 66 (73)69
Jan			

EQUIFORM™ Pg: 3   **DANCIN B B**   THE XTRAS™

Month	3	4	5
Dec	HU 61" 63(66)		
	HU =63" (58)=		
		M	
Nov	HU 64+ 64(70)		
	HU 62" ()63		
Oct	RE =-- ()=		
Sep	RE =-- ()=		
	RE =-- ()=		
Aug		EP 63" 61(68)66	
	M		
		EP 64 65(71)73	
Jul		LS 66 (70)70	
	LS 62+ 60(62)		
Jun		LS 65"w 62(65)	
		LS /61" 56(58)	
May	LS 64+ 60(65)	LS 65 61(65)	
		LS \66- (72)62	
	LS =67- (54)=	LS 66+ 63(68)	
Apr			-->
		HU /--w ()	
			SP 67 (71)72
Mar	HU 65-w 62(69)	HU -- ()	
			TP 65+ 62(66)58
	HU 63 60(64)	HU 63+ 61(67)57	
Feb			TP 69-w (75)71
	HU 64 56(58)	HU -- ()	
Jan	HU 60+ 55(57)	HU 65- 58(63)	

EQUIFORM™ Pg: 4   **AXE N ICE**   THE XTRAS™

4	5	6
TP 63" 61 (69) 70	TP 69+ 67 (76)	
TP /48 (63) 66		
	KD =:xx (61) =	
	EP 62" 65 (73)	
	CD 63 (73) 73	
	CD /65- 69 (82)	
	KE 66+ 68 (80) 77	
	TP 68" 70 (75)	-->
		TP 61" 68 (77)
	TP 60+ 65 (69)	
		TP 54+ (72) 72
	TP 67-w 70 (77)	
TP 62 63 (76) 75		
	TP 68- 70 (79)	
TP 63"w 62 (75) 78		

D e c N o v O c t S e p A u g J u l J u n M a y A p r M a r F e b J a n

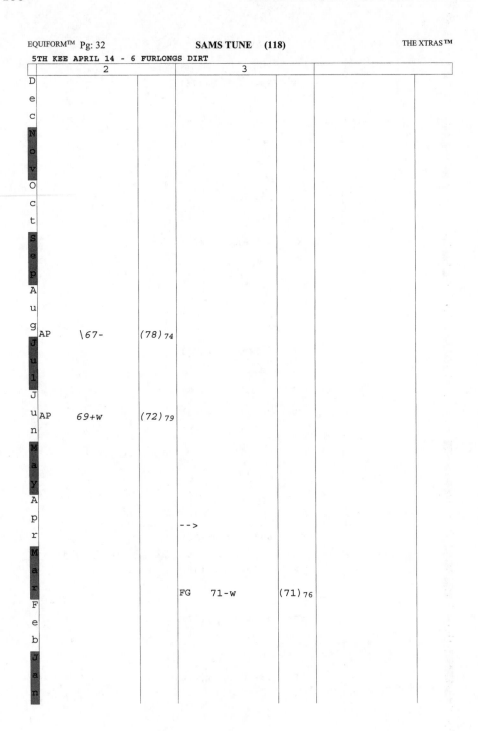

EQUIFORM™ Pg: 32   **SAMS TUNE   (118)**   THE XTRAS™

5TH KEE APRIL 14 - 6 FURLONGS DIRT

	2		3			
Dec						
Nov						
Oct						
Sep						
Aug						
Jul	AP	\67-	(78) 74			
Jun	AP	69+w	(72) 79			
May						
Apr			-->			
Mar			FG 71-w	(71) 76		
Feb						
Jan						

EQUIFORM™ Pg: 34   **CITY FAIR (118)**   THE XTRAS™

5TH KEE APRIL 14 - 6 FURLONGS DIRT

	2		3		
D	TP 69+w	67 (74) 69			
e					
c					
N					
o	CD 66	(78) 78			
v					
O	KE 65"	68 (80) 80			
c					
t	KE 68-	69 (86) 84			
S					
e					
p					
A					
u	MP ^68+	(74) 77			
g					
J					
u	MP /60"	(72) 73			
l					
J					
u					
n					
M					
a					
y					
A					
p			-->		
r					
M					
a					
r					
F			TP 66-	71 (81)	
e			TP /70-w	69 ()	
b					
J			TP ^62-	61 (72) 70	
a					
n					

Chapter 12

Oddments

Although touched upon earlier, the **back past performances** (BPP's) have several other applications. This chapter will address these along with some other concepts that don't fit neatly into any specific category.

Back Past Performances

With the exception of graded stakes, the *Racing Form* only displays a horse's last 10-12 races. Thus, its readers have little indication of the animal's performance or form cycles preceding those races. The career box may yield a clue, but it is no substitute for a careful look at these earlier efforts as they appear on **THE XTRAS**. By viewing a horse's last three years of performance, one may find evidence of certain cycles and patterns unavailable to the *Racing Form* reader. It could be a big final number 14 races back, a tendency to run a good race third time off a layoff when accompanied by a cyclical pace top, or a liking for a particular surface.

Take a look at the top two choices in the first race at Calder on December 31, 2000. In a five-horse field, two horses, Ronnies Answer at 4/5 and Minnie's Brat at 2/1, were vastly superior on raw figures (pages 163–164). Both were coming off layoffs, and Minnie's Brat had shown the ability to run some of her best numbers after a rest. Although I don't make a practice of betting 2/1 shots, Minnie's Brat was also getting almost two points in weight. I felt 2/1 warranted a wager, and she got up by a neck.

The BPP's are also useful in evaluating distance and surface switch-es when the horse's last ten or twelve races exhibit little or no variation along these lines. For example, a 5yo that has been routing over the last year is entered in a sprint. It may be just an exercise to sharpen his speed, but then again, the horse may be able to sprint successfully. The career box in the *Form* will show his best lifetime figure at the sprint distance, but that may have been earned as a 3yo, when he had not reached his full potential. The handicapper needs to know how those earlier sprint numbers stacked up against the route numbers he was running at that particular stage in his development. One can use the same reasoning to evaluate prior off track performances and surface switches.

The sixth race at the Fairgrounds on February 27, 2000, illustrates the BPP's in action again. The *Racing Form* only showed Cyrus's (page 165) last ten races, just missing the strong turf efforts he had run late in his 3yo season. Also note that two of his last three races featured dirt spreads of (-9), indicating his readiness for a return to the grass. The big favorite in the race, Yoto Speakes at 4/5, was nothing special, having run one 72 between three 69's in his last four races. Taking full advantage of the number one post, Cyrus received a rail-skimming ride and lit up the board at $49.20.

EQUIFORM™ Pg: 2   **RONNIES ANSWER   (116)**   THE XTRAS™

1ST CRC DECEMBER 31 - 5 1/2 FURLONGS DIRT

Month	2	3	4
Dec	CR /69" (77)$_{87}$	CR 69- (74)$_{80}$ CR 63- (74)$_{77}$	-->
Nov	CR 70"w (76)$_{77}$	CR 67+w (72)$_{76}$	
Nov	CR 58" (80)$_{82}$	CR 60" (66)$_{71}$	
Oct	CR 63- 67 (74)$_{74}$	CR 64 (75)$_{62}$	
Oct	CR 60 (78)$_{82}$	CR 65+ (80)$_{85}$	
Sep			
Aug	CR 67" (81)$_{90}$		CR /66 (75)$_{71}$
Aug	CR 64+w (76)$_{81}$	CR 68-w (74)$_{73}$ CR 58 (68)$_{84}$	CR 59+ 61 (77)$_{80}$
Jul		CR 64" 67 (73)$_{67}$	CR 64- (73)$_{83}$
Jun		CR 68+w (75)$_{83}$	CR 70+w (77)$_{82}$
Jun		CR 59" (76)$_{82}$	
May			CR 70"w (75)$_{76}$
Apr			GP 68 (76)$_{80}$
Mar			GP 66- (77)$_{82}$
Mar		GP 63+ (71)$_{75}$	
Feb			GP 71+ (82)$_{85}$
Jan		GP /65" (76)$_{85}$	
Jan		GP 67- (77)$_{81}$	

EQUIFORM™ Pg: 3   **MINNIE'S BRAT   (107*)**   THE XTRAS™

1ST CRC DECEMBER 31 - 5 1/2 FURLONGS DIRT

Month	6	7	8
D e c			-->
N o v			
O c t		BE \62+ (72) 69	
	ME /67" (76) 78	BE ^69" 68 (75) 78	
S e p	BE 53-60 (76) 79	CN 71w (78) 74	
A u g		SR 68 70 (79) 79	
J u l		MP 73"w (84) 83	
J u n		BE 73-w (80) 83	
M a y			DE 60" (72) 65
A p r			DE 67" (74) 74
		HI 59" (70) 75	
M a r		HI 71+ (72) 76	
	GP 72w 71 (76) 78		GP 70+w (76) 77
	GP 69 (79) 84	GP 72"w 72 (77) 76	
		GP 68+ 69 (77) 77	
F e b	GP >67" (77) 82		
J a n	GP 71"w (81) 82	GP 74-w 72 (75) 75	
	CR 73-w (82) 86		

EQUIFORM™ Pg: 41   **CYRUS (117)**   THE XTRAS™

6TH FGX FEBRUARY 27 STATE-BRED - 7 1/2 FURLONGS ABOUT TURF

Month	3	4	5
D	FG 69" 65 (67)		
e		FG 62- 59 (63)	
c	FG =72" (64)=		
N	FG =70- (61)=	FG 66+ 60 (60)	
o			
v			
O	LD /70- 55 (59)	LD =68- (70)=	
c			
t			
S			
e	LD 71 65 (63)		
p			
A	LD =61+ (62)=		
u			
g	LD 65" 59 (56)		
J			
u			
l			
J	LD =68 (54)=		
u			
n	PR 49+ 61 (64)		
M			
a	PR 67- 64 (61)		
y	PR 59- 61 (65)		
A			
p			
r			
M			
a		FG /67+ 65 (64)	
r		FG =70+ (64)=	
F		-->	FG 67+w 59 (58)
e			
b			FG /65 61 (63)
J	FG 59- 56 (59)		
a	FG 68w 59 (62)	FG 68+ 64 (66)	FG 67" 58 (58)
n			

The Sandwich or Surround

The BPP's lead us to another concept, the **sandwich** or **surround**. By looking at clusters of previous races, one can draw some key inferences. After seven dirt races, having reached a final top of 71-, Megans Bluff (page 167) tried the turf for the first time, and responded with a 73- over the Churchill Downs lawn. After a 70" dirt number at Thistledown, she reeled off three strong dirt performances at Arlington and Hoosier. When she returned to the grass in the Grade II Miss Revere Stakes on November 18 at Churchill, she made for an outstanding play. Most of the competition had recorded better grass figures than Megans Bluff's 73- (the rough equivalent of what one would see in the *Form's* career box). But the fact that she had run a 73- on the grass, sandwiched by two lower dirt numbers, showed she was capable of matching or exceeding her recent dirt numbers in the Miss Revere. I figured her to run about a 75", which was better than anybody in the race. Also, she rated to be the controlling speed, and rider Mark Guidry patiently guided her to a wire-to-wire win, returning $14.60.

EQUIFORM™ Pg: 1   **MEGANS BLUFF**   THE XTRAS™

	2		3		
D					
e					
c					
N					
o			-->		
v					
O					
c					
t			HR	$^{\wedge}77$	71 (71)
S	TP	67-	(73) 78		
e					
p			AP	75-w	74 (76)
A					
u			AP	75w	73 (77)
g					
J					
u			TD	$^{\wedge}70$"	68 (71)
l					
J	CD	69+	(80) 79 CD	=73-w	(68) =
u					
n					
M			CD	71-w	64 (67)
a					
y					
A			KE	71w	68 (74)
p					
r			KE	69+	61 (68)
M			GP	67-	(77) 80
a					
r			GP	69	68 (78) 83
F					
e					
b					
J					
a					
n					

Combos

Slew City Liz (page 169) exhibits the same type of pattern. Note how much better her initial grass efforts were when compared to the surrounding dirt races. When she returned to the turf on October 9, 2000, at Santa Anita, she had more than the "surround" in her favor. None of the favorites had run better than a 72" on the grass. In addition, she was receiving a positive jockey switch to Kent Desormeaux and more importantly, coming off a cyclical pace top on the dirt. Under a scintillating ride by Desormeaux, Slew City Liz closed with a rush to win by a nose at 13/1. These combination patterns or **combos** are very powerful.

Speaking of combos, we referred to one in an earlier chapter, that being the new dirt pace top followed by a reversal for a first time or lightly raced router. Above, we illustrated the sandwich accompanied by a cyclical pace top. Another good one is a new pace top with a recent good turnback number. Mybestsolution (4/1) was the third choice behind even money Double Character and Jettason (7/2) going six furlongs at Aqueduct on January 15, 2001 (pages 170−172). He was coming off a new pace top along with a 70 turnback number, and had run a 69 final as a 3yo. He won by a neck, paying $10.60.

Be on the lookout for these and other combination patterns.

EQUIFORM™ Pg: 1 **SLEW CITY LIZ (ONT-C)** THE XTRAS™

	2	3	4
D			
e			
c			
N			
o			
v			
O			
c			
t			-->
S			
e			DM 69+ $_{69}$(80)
p			
A			
u			
g			DM 64+ $_{60}$(64)
J			
u			
l			
J			GG =72- (69)=
u			
n			
M			HO =71 (68)=
a			
y			HO 67w (70)$_{75}$
A			
p			
r			SA 68"w $_{66}$(74)$_{79}$
M			SA 67 (71)$_{76}$
a			
r			
F			SA >69"w (80)$_{87}$
e			
b			SA 67 (78)$_{84}$
J			
a			
n			SA 67+ $_{66}$(80)$_{86}$

EQUIFORM™ Pg: 41   **MYBESTSOLUTION   (117)**   THE XTRAS™

6TH AQU JANUARY 15   STATE-BRED - 6 FURLONGS INNER DIRT

	2	3	4
D			
e			
c			
N			
o		AQ 65+ 68 (71)	
v			
O			
c			
t		BE ^68- 62 (62)	
S			
e			
p			
A		SR 67+w 57 (59)	
u			
g			
J			
u		BE 69 67 (70)	
l			
J		BE 65- 64 (73) 76	
u			
n		BE 63- (56) 39	
M			
a			
y			
A			
p			
r			
M			
a			
r			
F			
e			
b			
J			-->
a			
n			AQ 66" 70 (79)

EQUIFORM™ Pg: 48   **JETTASON (122)**   THE XTRAS™

6TH AQU JANUARY 15   STATE-BRED - 6 FURLONGS INNER DIRT

	2	3		4
D		AQ 67+	(76) 76	
e		AQ /66+w	(78) 80	
c				
N		AQ 66+	(76) 80	
o				
v		AQ 63+	(72) 77	
O				
c				
t		BE 61+ 60	(67) 70	
S				
e				
p				
A				
u				
g		SR \62+ 62	(74) 75	
J				
u		BE /63	(71) 62	
l				
J				
u				
n				
M				
a				
y				
A				
p				
r				
M				
a				
r				
F				
e				
b				
J				
a		-->		
n				

EQUIFORM™ Pg: 47   **DOUBLE CHARACTER (117)**   THE XTRAS™

6TH AQU JANUARY 15   STATE-BRED - 6 FURLONGS INNER DIRT

	2		3		4
Dec	AQ 65"	(77) 82	AQ 68w	(76) 80	
e					
c AQ	64	(77) 84	AQ 62-	(75) 69	
Nov					
Oct					
Sep					
Aug					
Jul					
Jun					
May			BE 68- 69	(79) 81	
			BE 67+ 70	(82) 82	
y			**AQ 65+ 71**	**(82)**	
Apr			AQ 64w	(81) 86	
r			AQ 60"	(76) 79	
Mar			AQ /69"	(75) 75	
a			**AQ 52+ 66**	**(71)**	
r			**AQ 63 62**	**(67)**	
Feb			AQ 60"	(71) 73	
e				-->	
b **J**an			AQ 64	(78) 88	

Equipment Changes

Equipment changes can often be the precursor of dramatic form reversals. In my opinion, blinker changes are generally misunderstood. The public and some otherwise astute handicappers assume that the addition of blinkers shows immediate positive intent. That may be, but then again, the trainer may be using them only as an experiment to focus the animal's attention. In fact, trainer statistics in the *Racing Form* indicate that the vast majority of trainers have a lower winning percentage with first time blinkers than their overall percentage.

On average, trainers do better with second time blinkers. For most horses, it takes some time to get accustomed to "the hood". Imagine a football quarterback who could only see a slice of the field. Blinkers would help him focus on hitting his downfield receiver. But, with limited peripheral vision, he would be much more vulnerable to crushing blows from defensive players that "blindside" him.

Getting bumped and jostled by other horses they can't see isn't a pleasant experience for most racehorses. If the focusing aspect of blinkers helps an animal get better early position, they may have a positive effect. Even though they may have had workouts with the blinkers on (required in most jurisdictions), most horses require a race or two to acclimate to the new equipment.

There are several different types of blinkers (full cups, half cups, etc), and a trainer may try different ones in an effort to ascertain the individual horse's preference.

Although blinkers on or blinkers off are the most common equipment change, there are several others. Aluminum pads, bar shoes, mud caulks, no whip, earmuffs, and the ultimate equipment change, first time gelding, can also impact a horse's performance. Judging the probable effect of these changes is not a science, and the best method to evaluate them is to study the particular trainer's ability in these situations.

Above The Harbor (page 175) began her career with two solid sprint races at Delaware Park, and then threw in a clunker going two turns for the first time. Trainer Robert Camac added blinkers in her next start, and she had worn the new equipment ever since, including her last three starts for new trainer Del Carroll. On March 14, 2001, in the third race at Aqueduct, Carroll removed the blinkers.

Holly Jolly, coming off two sup-par efforts in stakes, was the odds-on favorite, with Polly Moon (7/2) as the second choice (see pages 176−177). I was amazed to see Above The Harbor at 9/1. She was coming off successive new pace tops and had run her two best races without blinkers. The blinkers were coming off now, and so was the rubber band on my bankroll. Above The Harbor sped to the lead and withstood the late charge of Maria's Crown to win by a half-length.

EQUIPMENT CHANGES

3RD AQU MARCH 14 - 7 FURLONGS DIRT

Month	2		3		
Dec	SU \68w	(75) 80			
Nov	LR /65"	(71) 76			
Oct	DE 64"	(71) 80			
Ct	DE 54" 65	(67)			
Sep	DE 61" 63	(65)			
Aug	DE 69-	(72) 70			
g	DE 70	(75) 77			
Jul					
Jun					
May					
Apr					
Mar			-->		
Feb			SU 65	(78) 82	
Jan			AQ 63-	(76) 78	

EQUIFORM™ Pg: 21   **HOLLY JOLLY   (120)**   THE XTRAS™

3RD AQU MARCH 14 - 7 FURLONGS DIRT

2	3		
LR 70w 68 (76) 80			
LR 70+w (72) 70			
LR 66 65 (73) 71			
LR 65- (71) 74			
DE 62- (71) 73			
	-->		
	CT 65" 67 (69) 65		
	PH 66+ (80) 87		
	LR 71+w 70 (73) 76		

D
e
c
N
o
v
O
c
t
S
e
p
A
u
g
J
u
l
J
u
n
M
a
y
A
p
r
M
a
r
F
e
b
J
a
n

EQUIFORM™ Pg: 18   **POLLY MOON**   **(118)**   THE XTRAS™

3RD AQU MARCH 14 - 7 FURLONGS DIRT

	2		3		
D e c	AQ 68"	(75) 80			
N o v	AQ 61-	(71) 77			
	ME \64-	(72) 72			
O c t					
S e p	WO 66"w	(78) 75			
	WO 64"	68 (81) 84			
A u g					
J u l	WO 70-w	(75) 84			
J u n					
M a y					
A p r					
M a r			-->		
F e b			AQ 66-	63 (69)	
J a n			AQ ^66"	(76) 77	

Excuses

Some astounding payoffs can be had by the careful analysis and interpretation of excuses in the running lines, and The Xtras can often help the handicapper uncover these nuggets.

The key to this exercise is to be totally objective. Wide trip, stumbled start, blocked, shut off, steadied, and my favorite, buck jumped, are just a few of the plethora of excuses that clutter the comment lines in every issue of the *Racing Form*. Determining when these excuses really are important and provide wagering value is not an easy task. Blocked, steadied, and boxed-in are probably the most overrated trouble lines. Unless a horse's momentum is severely compromised, the minimal restraint necessitated by these situations is often not decisive. In fact, sometimes it can work to the horse's advantage by preventing it from getting involved in a speed duel or by allowing it to conserve a little energy on a track favoring closers.

The wide comments are also ambiguous. No two chart-callers see a race quite the same way. One caller's four wide may be another's seven wide. And were they four wide for the whole turn, or just fanning wide as they entered the stretch? Was the outside part of the track good, bad or neutral? Was it four wide on the tight turns at Pimlico or four wide on the sweeping turns at Belmont Park? Does a particular animal seem to record its best numbers when allowed to run in the clear, outside of other horses? Until you know the answers to these questions, don't put too much emphasis on wide comments.

As I studied the eleventh and final race at Gulfstream Park on March 11, 2001, a maiden special weight race for three-year-olds, I noticed four horses were coming off new pace tops. Two of these were off extended layoffs, and one was off a double top, but the fourth one, Built Up, had raced just three weeks earlier while making a nine point pace move in his second career start. As I delved deeper into the PP's, I saw that Built Up had been checked and bumped at the break in his debut while running a 64/62" compression line. Then, in his second attempt, he met a similar fate, earning a 73/62+. It is difficult to assess whether these kinds of mishaps are genuinely bad racing luck or just poor breaking tendencies specific to the particular horse.

As I glimpsed Built Up at 60/1 on the tote board, another clue emerged. The heavy favorite in the race at 6/5 was Bat Runner. Despite checking at the start from the outside post on February 17, Built Up had been only 1-1/2 lengths behind Bat Runner after four furlongs. I felt that this showed he wasn't completely overmatched, and started constructing some plays using Built Up. Unfortunately, most of my investment had him in the second and third slots, so that when he waltzed home at $200.20, all I collected was a small win/place bet. I was a little disappointed that I hadn't put more on the nose, but thankful that the new pace top had pointed me in the right direction.

Drawing an outside post position can often be a major obstacle, especially for a speed horse negotiating two turns in a large field. These front-running types use a lot of energy trying to "clear" and get to the top, and if confronted with other speed from the inside, are often hung wide on the clubhouse turn while batting for the lead. This is a difficult setup to overcome, and often leads to a severe fade later in the race as the jockey realizes there is no hope. But when these same horses return and draw an inside post in a race without much early lick, the result can be quite different.

Even in sprints, an inside draw, coupled with a tactical pace advantage can be very advantageous. Look at Marketchase in the fifth race at Gulfsteam Park on March 5, 2001 (page 180). After breaking from the eleven post in a route in her 6yo debut, Marketchase moved to the inside in her next start and won at 8/1. Stepped up a notch in class, she was entered again at seven furlongs, drawing the two post. My Guy Norman, in the one hole, was a stone closer, and Marketchase was coming off a cyclical pace top (80) with the best recent pace number in the race. She emerged victorious again, paying $15.60.

EQUIFORM™ Pg: 34   **MARKETCHASE   (116)**   THE XTRAS™

5TH GPX MARCH 5 - 7 FURLONGS DIRT

Month	4	5	6
Dec	CR 64 65 (76) 81		
Nov	ME 73"w 70 (78)		
Oct	ME 72- 69 (76)	ME 67"w 65 (74)	
Oct	ME 70 71 (80)	ME 65+ 68 (78)	
		ME 68-w 66 (76)	
Sep	ME 68" (74) 77	ME 65 65 (75)	
		ME 62" (78) 83	
Aug	MP /68- (77) 79		
Jul	MP 70" (78) 77		
Jul	MP 69+w (77) 78		
Jun		MP 58- 67 (79)	
Jun	MP 65 (79) 85		
May	MP 47+ (66) 78	MP 62+ (73) 80	
Apr		GP /65- (69) 79	
Mar		GP 65 65 (75) 78	
Mar		GP 65" 66 (73) 80	
			-->
Feb		GP 59- 68 (72)	GP 68w 69 (80) 88
Feb		GP 61" 66 (70)	
Jan		GP 70+ 66 (67)	GP 62- 61 (68)

Soft Wins

It is sometimes tricky to evaluate a horse when a victory is earned with an "off" final number. A **soft win** occurs when a horse wins a race with *both* its pace and final numbers below its recent bests. Look at Miss Vermont Jet (page 182) as she appeared in the third race at Hialeah on April 9, 2001. She had some competitive final figures, and although she won her previous race, it had come off a precipitous drop to the $5,000 level on March 17. The 73 pace number and the 64- final number she recorded in that March 17 win were both well below the 77 pace and 68- final she had run in her last dirt race. She also had a 77/69- back in January. The weaker numbers on March 17 were all she had to run to win that particular race. Miss Vermont Jet probably could have run faster that day, but the *softer* company did not require it (why win by eight lengths when two will suffice).

Miss Vermont Jet was claimed out of the March 17 race by trainer Henry Collazo. The public didn't fully appreciate that Collazo had "called the bluff" on the big drop to $5,000, and was now exhibiting his confidence by jacking her right back up the ladder to $25,000. The soft win had partially concealed her true condition, and Miss Vermont Jet eked out a victory at 9/1.

Now look at Until Sundown (page 183). After running a compression line of 78/75 in his debut, he ran a 72/70+ when stretched to a route in his second start, and broke his maiden by a comfortable four lengths. This soft win should take nothing away from his ability to equal or exceed his opening effort in his first start versus winners. On April 11, 2001, Until Sundown showed up in a NW1 at one mile at Santa Anita. That opening 75 laid over the field, and he responded with another facile win at 9/5.

EQUIFORM™ Pg: 17   **MISS VERMONT JET   (116)**   THE XTRAS™

3RD HIA APRIL 9 - 6 FURLONGS DIRT

Month	2	3	4
D		CR 56+ (64) 79	
e			
c		CR /68+ (74) 83	
N		CR 65"w (73) 82	
o			
v		CR 62" (72) 86	
O			
c			
t	CR =66+ (81) =		
S	CR /62- 68 (81)		
e			
p			
A			
u	CR /68-w (77) 80		
g			
J	CR 66"w (72) 73		
u			
l			
J			
u			
n			
M			
a			
y			
A			
p			
r		-->	
M			
a			HI 64-w (73) 80
r			GP =64- (68) =
F			GP 68- (77) 81
e			
b			
J			GP 54" (69) 71
a			
n			GP 69- (77) 82

UNTIL SUNDOWN (121)

DIRT

	3	
-->		
SA	70+w	65 (72)
SA	75	74 (78) 78

SHARELYN'S GOLD (122)

BRED - 6 FURLONGS DIRT

	3	
-->		
AQ	64+	62 (70) 75
AQ	69-w	(78) 80
AQ	66+	(74) 77
AQ	61"	(71) 65

EQUIFORM™ Pg: 39   **JUST JUSTIN (117)**

5TH AQU APRIL 19   STATE-BRED - 6 FURLONGS DIRT

	2		3	
u	SR 67w	(71) 74		
g	SR /61"	(68) 65		
			-->	
P				
r			AQ 66	66 (73) 77

EQUIFORM™ Pg: 32   **BROCCO BOB (117)**

5TH AQU APRIL 19   STATE-BRED - 6 FURLONGS DIRT

	2		3	
u	SR 66	67 (79) 79		
g	SR /67-w	(76) 85		
u	BE 57"	(60) 52		
P			-->	
r				
N			AQ 67+	66 (76) 79
a				

Bests

Over the years, we've found a mechanical method that produces consistent profits. The selections generated by this method don't occur very often, but are nice spot plays to have in one's arsenal. The rules are simple. Look at the last three final numbers (on today's surface) of all the entrants that have raced within the last 60 days. If the horse with the best final number in the last three races is 10/1 or better, make a bet. The 10/1 cut-off is used for average field sizes. In small fields (six horses or less), we accept 8/1, but demand 12/1 if more than ten horses are running.

The fifth race at Aqueduct on April 19, 2001, at six furlongs, matched seven 3yo New York bred colts (three of which appear on page 183). On The Xtras, it looked like a competitive race, with each horse having some chance. But for whatever reason, the crowd zeroed in on Just Justin (2/1) and Brocco Bob (5/2).

When looking at the last three final numbers of each horse, Sharelyn's Gold's 69- was tied for top prize with Secret Pro (5/1). She had bounced to a 64+ off that double top, but when I saw her at 12/1 a couple minutes to post, I had a **best** play. It's not often that one gets this kind of price on a Scott Lake horse with decent numbers. After Sharelyn's Gold rallied to win, I still didn't understand why he had been such a big price, but $30.40 was music to my ears.

As mentioned, these plays don't occur that frequently, but in the ninth race on that same Aqueduct card, another best play surfaced. Miz Koddington (page 185) is the kind of horse most handicappers, including me, give the immediate heave-ho. Five year old mares that are 0/21 with weak connections hardly inspire confidence. But, Miz Koddington's 62" three races back was best. In addition, she had a forward going pattern until her last race, when she stumbled at the start. She also had decent pace ability, which is always a plus in weak state-bred races. In fact, she was on a pretty good line, a **delayed cyclical pace top**. Did I bet her? No. Should I have? Yes. Under time pressure, I hadn't noticed the poor break in her last effort or that she had run a cyclical pace top two back. Still, I should have played her on the best theory. It is difficult to break old thought processes, even for people who know better.

EQUIFORM™ Pg: 77 **MIZ KODDINGTON   (122)** THE XTRAS™

9TH AQU APRIL 19   STATE-BRED - 6 FURLONGS DIRT

Month	3		4		5	
Dec	AQ 58+	(73) 77	AQ 56"	(70) 64		
Nov			AQ /60-	(70) 76		
Nov	**AQ 54** 58 **(69)**		AQ 56	(65) 75		
Nov			AQ 58"	(73) 78		
Oct	AQ 63-	(75) 81				
Oct			BE 58	(71) 67		
Sep			BE 60-	(69) 71		
Aug						
Jul						
Jun	BE 62-	(70) 73	BE 54"	(66) 64		
May	BE 64+	(69) 73				
Apr			-->			
Mar			AQ 51+ 54	(76) 84		
Mar			AQ \63	(75) 76	AQ 57"	(70) 72
Feb					AQ ^62	(75) 73
Feb			AQ 57-	(73) 73	AQ 62"	(72) 74
Feb					AQ 59	(72) 75
Jan			AQ 62	(73) 71	AQ 57-	(72) 78

Chapter 13

At the Windows

The ultimate test of handicapping skill is making decisions under pressure with real money on the line. Both intense preparation and good organizational skills are necessary, especially for simulcast players perusing several tracks. **THE XTRAS** provide superior information that enhances the handicapper's ability to predict performance and establish fair odds. After that, it is up to the player to construct bets that suit his wagering style and temperament.

With hindsight, it's always easy to say that you could have had that last winner if only you had noticed a certain piece of information. In most races, a case can be made for several horses. The only way to decide which, if any, are worth a wager is to estimate each contender's true probability of winning, and only bet those offering attractive odds. Don't get upset if you make your top choice 2/1, and he wins at 8/5. Remember, if your line is accurate, your 2/1 shots will win one out of three times, and you must learn to let them win without you when the price isn't right.

When contemplating a wager, ask yourself if you know something that is obscured from the public. The Xtras often furnish the clues that allow one to find horses that are in good condition *and* offer value.

Even then, amidst the crush of information, it is easy for simulcast players to lose focus. While monitoring the exacta prices at the Fairgrounds, one might lose sight of the four horse at Aqueduct blowing out from 6/1 to 10/1 in the last couple minutes before post. When the

$22.40 payoff flashes on the board, it's time to take a cue from Minnesota Fats and freshen up. One cannot handicap or wager properly if frustrated or tired. When I start feeling like this, I take a walk or pass a few races to get my head straight again.

By studying the examples in this book, you will gain a better understanding of thoroughbred condition. But as we all know, examples are one thing, reality is quite another. That's not to say that some plays don't jump off the page, but rather that the player is usually confronted with more complex situations. The second race at Aqueduct on December 27, 2000, exemplifies this kind of race. No fewer than four horses were coming off new pace tops in this claiming sprint for three-year-olds and, only after a thorough analysis, did I make a wager.

After beginning his career with four attempts in maiden special weight events, Olerud (page 191) was dropped into a $50,000 maiden claimer going seven furlongs on September 10 at Belmont Park. He won that race and in his next start faced $35,000, 3yo claimers. His final number of 65 in the maiden claiming victory was below his previous top of 67. On the Beyer speed scale, he had run a 56, versus a high of 62. What was coming next? The (79) pace number, along with the two furlong improvement to an 83, gives **EQUIFORM** players a big clue. The new pace top, coupled with an "off" final number, created an excellent betting opportunity. As further evidence of Olerud's concealed condition, note how his six-furlong turnback numbers on September 3 and 10 (66 and 68) were buried inside of slower seven-furlong final numbers. The public had little idea this was an improving animal, which would be competitive facing winners for the first time. Olerud exploded to a 72" paying $20.00.

Stepped up to $50,000 in his next start, Olerud bounced big time, as expected. He returned after a 25-day hiatus (his longest rest period to that point) on Nov 15 and bounced back with a creditable 69-, showing that the effect of the 72" top was beginning to wear off. On December 10, entered for $25,000 again, the new (82) pace top signaled he was ready for another good effort. The 70 final number that accompanied this pace top was below his previous top, indicating there was a good chance he could approach or even exceed that 72" in his next race.

In his last three races, Olerud had finished third, beaten 4-1/2 lengths, sixth by 6 lengths, and seventh by 22-1/4 lengths and his recent form looked sketchy. The crowd made Gator Go Getter (page 192) the chalk at 2-1. Trained by the redoubtable Scott Lake, this gelding had run first or second in four of his last five races while recording strong Beyer numbers. He was also off a new pace top, but had curiously been laid off for over a month. For a gelding in supposedly good form, this is usually not a good sign. In addition, Gator Go Getter showed only one workout since his last race, a slow four furlong move at Philadelphia Park two weeks earlier. This is not the kind of animal you want to take at 2-1.

It was a tough race but, at 7/1, I thought Olerud offered some value and wagered accordingly. After being pinched at the start, Olerud rallied wide and got up by a nose, with Gator Go Getter off the board.

The fourth race at Aqueduct on March 10, 2001 provided a wonderful example of using The Xtras (pages 193–194), along with a little imagination, to land some exceptional payoffs. When I glanced at the mile race over the inner track, I noticed that Thisbirdsforyou was coming off a big new pace top, with a couple of 65 finals as a foundation. When I saw 20/1 on the morning line, I delved deeper. The program choice at 2/1 was Tell Me True, a Ben Perkins Jr trainee who had run a negative spread of 74/67- in his only race. He was clearly worth betting against, and there were some other interesting contenders.

Classic Endeavor had been haltered for $75,000 by Scott Schwartz on September 2, 2000, at Saratoga. That claim struck a chord, as very few maidens are claimed for such a pricey tag. If Classic Endeavor could run a 66" as a September 2yo, and Schwartz was willing to shell out $75,000, I reasoned there was a decent chance he could run a 67 or 68. Patriot American also had a nice look, coming off a new pace top, but had slower finals than Classic Endeavor and Thisbirdsforyou.

As they approached the starting gate, Tell Me True was a ridiculous 6/5, with Classic Endeavor 10/1, and Thisbirdsforyou 30/1. I made sizable win/place bets on both of the latter, boxed them in the exacta, and also made smaller exacta boxes combining those two with Patriot American. As the prices below illustrate, I was amply rewarded. But in the last minute rush, I had made a mistake. Normally not a fan of the triple and its exorbitant 25% take, this was a race that screamed for one. With a vulnerable favorite who could be off the board, the payoff could be nice, even in this short field. After patting myself on the back for collecting a $443 exacta, I looked at the television screen and saw that Patriot American had run third to complete a $2,131 triple.

Fourth Race, Aqueduct, March 10, 2001

Horse	Win	Place	Show
2 Classic Endeavor	24.20	12.60	7.90
7 Thisbirdsforyou		20.20	6.50
4 Patriot American			4.80
$2 Exacta 2-7 paid $443			
$2 Triple 2-7-4 paid $2131			

This game is never easy.

EQUIFORM™ Pg: 19   **OLERUD   (118)**   THE XTRAS™

2ND AQU DECEMBER 27 - 6 FURLONGS INNER DIRT

	2		3		
D e c		-->			
N o v		AQ	70		(82) 80
O c t		AQ	69-		(73) 62
S e p		BE	62		(76) 81
		BE	72"w		(79) 85
A u g		BE	65w	68	(79) 83
		SR	62+	66	(76) 78
J u l		SR	67	68	(76) 78
		SR	**=^63"**		**(59) =**
		SR	59"		(67) 50
J u n					
M a y					
A p r					
M a r					
F e b					
J a n					

EQUIFORM™ Pg: 22   **GATOR GO GETTER   (118)**   THE XTRAS™

2ND AQU DECEMBER 27 - 6 FURLONGS INNER DIRT

Month	2			3		
D	CR	68+w	(80)84	-->		
e	CR	65"w	(74)78			
c						
N	CR	59+	(67)66	PH	70"	(85)89
o	CR	64+ 66	(72)69	ME	/66-	(74)75
v						
O	CR	58	(75)82			
c						
t	CR	55" 58	(67)70	PH	68"w	(81)80
S	CR	57	(64)60	PH	/71+	(80)84
e						
p				PH	70+ 70	(83)82
A				MP	=^59+	(64)=
u						
g						
J						
u				MP	=62"	(72)=
l				MP	=64	(63)=
J						
u						
n						
M				BE	=^63-	(65)=
a						
y				GP	=68-	(62)=
A						
p				GP	=67-	(53)=
r						
M						
a						
r						
F				GP	56"	(68)78
e				GP	xx	(70)73
b						
J						
a				GP	62" 63	(79)87
n						

EQUIFORM™ Pg: 23   **CLASSIC ENDEAVOR**   (120)

4TH AQU MARCH 10 - 1 MILE INNER DIRT

	2		3	
P	SR 59+	(66) 60		
A				
u				
g	SR /66"	(71) 72		
J				

EQUIFORM™ Pg: 24   **WEEKEND HONOR**   (120)

4TH AQU MARCH 10 - 1 MILE INNER DIRT

	2		3	
N	TP 67-	(75) 78		
o				
v				
O	CD 65"	(74) 76		
c				
r		-->		
F			AQ 63+	(66) 67
e				
b				
J				
a				
n			GP 66+ 67 (78) 81	

EQUIFORM™ Pg: 25   **PATRIOT AMERICAN**   (120)

4TH AQU MARCH 10 - 1 MILE INNER DIRT

	2		3	
r			-->	
F			AQ 63" 67	(72)
e				
b			AQ 62+	(69) 5

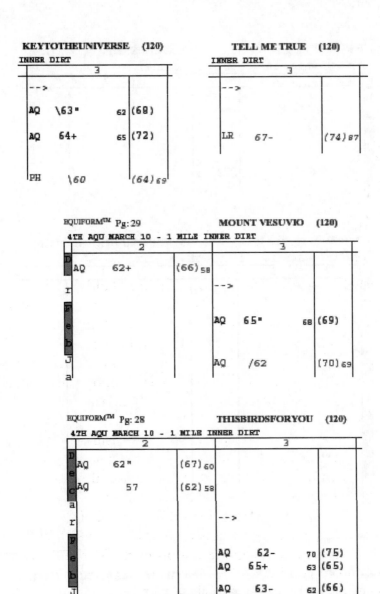

KEYTOTHEUNIVERSE   (120)

INNER DIRT

	3	
-->		
AQ \63"	62	(69)
AQ 64+	65	(72)
PH \60		(64) 69

TELL ME TRUE   (120)

INNER DIRT

	3	
-->		
LR 67-		(74) 87

EQUIFORM™ Pg: 29   **MOUNT VESUVIO   (120)**

4TH AQU MARCH 10 - 1 MILE INNER DIRT

	2		3	
D AQ	62+	(66) 58		
r			-->	
u			AQ 65"	68 (69)
e b J a			AQ /62	(70) 69

EQUIFORM™ Pg: 28   **THISBIRDSFORYOU   (120)**

4TH AQU MARCH 10 - 1 MILE INNER DIRT

	2		3	
D AQ	62"	(67) 60		
e c AQ	57	(62) 58		
a r			-->	
g			AQ 62-	70 (75)
e			AQ 65+	63 (65)
b			AQ 63-	62 (66)
J a			AQ 65	64 (66)

Coda

"The rarest of human qualities is an open mind"
CHARTS

The truth of the mantra of my late gambling buddy, Charts, was apparent when I first formulated the theories that are the crux of **THE XTRAS**. In the beginning, only a limited number of people showed any interest at all, and fewer still recognized their potential. Several of these initial reviewers were "sheet" players. But they were reluctant to accept that there might be a better way, to move on to something new. The only person to show any sustained inquisitiveness was Richie Schwartz.

Richie made a fortune in the '70s and '80s using the "sheets", but he realized that the big edge he once enjoyed had been eroded, another victim of the pari-mutuel system. He knew also that to continue winning, he had to find a different information set.

Although we share a passion for bridge (Richie has won four major national championships), handicapping is our first love. Over the years, Richie assisted in designing the product. More importantly, he encouraged me to continue my research. He may not know as much about The Xtras as I do, but he knows a lot more about winning.

I have gambled most of my life. Whether it was flipping coins in grade school, playing poker and the horses through college, or trading currencies as an adult, the gaming life has allowed me to meet some fascinating and wonderful characters along the way. None of them was as good a pure gambler as Richie. Through focus, intense determination and a natural affinity for numbers, he knows how to "get the money". His keen judgment and impeccable last minute betting instincts have improved my game considerably.

About Cary Fotias

Cary Fotias, President and Founder of **EQUIFORM**, is a throwback to the '50s and '60s gaming markets professional. His passion for mathematical games, including bridge, poker, blackjack, and currency trading is based on a firm grasp of fundamentals and the inherent statistical relationships implied during any point in play. Cary received a BA from the University of Michigan and an MBA from Indiana University. After a few years of full time poker and eight years of trading currencies on Wall Street, Cary has spent the last ten years as a professional handicapper. Over that time, he founded Equiform to enable him to conduct advanced research into the performance and form cycles of thoroughbred racehorses.

Cary does not merely participate in a game, but attacks it from many angles simultaneously. A highly developed sense of valuation allows him to structure wagers in combinations that give his investments superior risk/reward characteristics. Cary's play and confidence arise from intense focus and preparation along with 30 years of gaming and markets experience. On race day, he calculates with the rapid-fire intuition of the old style pro who, every so often, might also use a pad and pencil. In thoroughbred racing, considered by many the toughest of all games to beat, Cary continues to excel. While few can match his historic knowledge of the sport, he succeeds today due to dedication, innovation and constant study. Cary also takes special pride in his ability to explain intricate concepts clearly and concisely. Nowhere are these traits more evident than in our leading product, **THE XTRAS**.

NEW YORK CITY December 2001